ULTIMATE COLLECTION OF PRO HOCKEY RECORDS 2015

BY SHANE FREDERICK

capstone
young readers

Sports Illustrated Kids Ultimate Collection of Pro Hockey Records 2015
is published by Capstone Young Readers,
1710 Roe Crest Drive, North Mankato, Minnesota 56003.
www.capstonepub.com

Copyright © 2015 by Capstone Young Readers, a Capstone imprint.
All rights reserved. No part of this publication may be reproduced in whole or in part, or stored in a retrieval system, or transmitted in any form or by any means, electronic, mechanical, photocopying, recording, or otherwise, without written permission of the publisher. For information regarding permission, write to Capstone Young Readers,
1710 Roe Crest Drive, North Mankato, Minnesota 56003.

SI Kids is a trademark of Time Inc. Used with permission.

Library of Congress Cataloging-in-Publication Data
Cataloging-in-publication information is on file with the Library of Congress.

ISBN 978-1-4914-1962-5

Edited by Clare Lewis and Anthony Wacholtz
Designed by Richard Parker and Eric Manske
Media Research by Eric Gohl
Production by Helen McCreath

Photo Credits
123RF: Rocco Macri, 98; AP Images: The Canadian Press, 76, Paul Connors, 113t; Corbis: Bettmann, 120t, Underwood & Underwood, 43b; Dreamstime: Jerry Coli, cover (right); Getty Images: Bruce Bennett Studios, 21b, 29b, 73, 77b, 78b, 79t, 94b, 105t, 112, NHLI/Denis Brodeur, 36t, 67b, NHLI/Steve Babineau, 22b, 34b, 69; Library of Congress: 124t; Newscom: Ai Wire/Randy Wilson, 118b, Icon SMI/IHA, 42b, 95b, Icon SMI/John Cordes, 47, iPhoto Inc./Dave Abel, 24, iPhoto Inc./Dennis Miles, 92t, KRT/Huy Nguyen, 117b, KRT/Roy Gallop, 15b, Louis Deluca, 110b, MCT/Ralph Lauer, 111, UPI Photo Service/Bill Pugliano, 67t, UPI Photo Service/Michael Bush, 23b; Shutterstock: Fahrner, 105b, Marty Ellis, 60–61 (background), 113b, Nip, 8–9, Rob Marmion, 10–11, Zeliksone Veronika, 62t; Sports Illustrated: Bob Martin, 102b, Bob Rosato, 25b, 26t, 40, 49t, 55bl, 79b, 95t, Damian Strohmeyer, 14b, 16–17, 25t, 35t, 37, 46, 49b, 57bl, 82, 121t, 121b, David E. Klutho, cover (left), 2m, 2b, 3, 4¬–5, 6, 9t, 9br, 11t, 13, 14t, 18, 19t, 20t, 21t, 22t, 23t, 27t, 33t, 36b, 42t, 43t, 44, 45b, 50b, 51t, 51bmr, 52b, 53ml, 53mr, 54r, 55bmr, 56t, 57bml, 57bmr, 57br, 60r, 61t, 61m, 62b, 63t, 64–65, 66, 70, 71, 78t, 80–81, 84t, 85b, 86b, 87b, 89, 90, 91t, 91b, 93t, 93b, 94t, 96t, 97, 99, 100t, 103t, 103b, 104l, 104r, 107t, 107b, 108t, 108b, 109t, 109m, 109b, 114–115, 120b, 123, 125, Heinz Kluetmeier, 77b, 85t, 102t, Hy Peskin, 12, 48, 51bl, 51br, 55t, 63b, 86t, 92b, 100b, 119r, John D. Hanlon, 2t, 32, 33b, 52m, 59t, 101, John G. Zimmerman, 55br, 118t, John Iacono, 74t, 83t, 124b, Lane Stewart, 84b, Manny Millan, 26b, 28, 31, 53r, 60l, 68b, 88, Richard Meek, 19b, 50t, 83t, Robert Beck, 7, 27b, 45t, 52t, 56b, 57t, 58b, 87b, 106, 110t, 116, Simon Bruty, 38–39, Tony Triolo, cover (middle), 15t, 20b, 29t, 30, 34t, 35b, 41, 51bml, 53l, 54l, 55bml, 58t, 59b, 61b, 68t, 74b, 117t, 119l, Walter Iooss Jr., 75, Wikimedia: Kendrick Erickson, 96b, spcbrass, 72

Design Elements
Shutterstock: ArtyFree, B Calkins, Dusty Cline, fmua, ssuaphotos

Printed in Canada.
092014   007105

TABLE OF CONTENTS

INTRODUCTION 4

CHAPTER 1
THE GAME 6

CHAPTER 2
SKATER RECORDS 16

CHAPTER 3
GOALTENDER RECORDS 38

CHAPTER 4
PLAYERS 50

CHAPTER 5
TEAM RECORDS 64

CHAPTER 6
THE TEAMS 70

CHAPTER 7
PLAYOFF RECORDS 80

CHAPTER 8
FAN FAVORITES 96

CHAPTER 9
GREATEST MOMENTS 108

CHAPTER 10
RINK RECORDS 114

TIMELINE 124
READ MORE 126
INTERNET SITES 126
INDEX 127

INTRODUCTION

It's easy to see why enthusiasm surrounds hockey. The sport has speed and skill, hard hits, and intensity. Game-winning goals are celebrated with group hugs, and even the fiercest rivals line up and shake hands after a grueling playoff series. Each game opens the possibility for an amazing goal or a shocking check into the boards.

The game of hockey has been fiercely competitive ever since 1892, for it was then that Lord Frederick Arthur Stanley, Governor General of Canada, donated a trophy for the purposes of deciding the best hockey team in the land. The Stanley Cup, as it came to be known, was subsequently highly sought after by the best players and teams. It is still awarded

▼ 2013 Stanley Cup Champion Chicago Blackhawks

each season to the top team in the National Hockey League (NHL).

Another way to decide the best of the best through the ages is by keeping records. Setting a record is a big deal. It's a historic event. A record establishes a player or team as one of the greats in contrast to others and is used as a measuring stick for young and future players.

Hockey today is as colorful, competitive, and exciting as it's ever been. The pages that follow represent the finest players, teams, and feats that the dazzling sport of hockey has ever seen.

Chapter 1: THE GAME

LET'S PLAY HOCKEY

The play begins with a bone-crushing hit. The defenseman drives the opposing puck carrier into the boards, rattling the glass. He scoops up the puck as his victim falls to the ice. The defenseman passes it ahead to a forward flying through the neutral zone. The forward catches the puck and makes a fancy move to get around a defender. He fakes a shot during the breakaway to get the goalie moving. He follows the fake with a rocket shot that sends the puck over the goalie's shoulder and into the net. Goal!

A big hit, a beautiful pass, a crazy deke, and a goal. It's the perfect combination to send any crowd into a frenzy, whether it's at a city rink, a high school arena, or a 20,000-seat NHL stadium.

THE EVOLUTION OF HOCKEY

The game of hockey that we know today looked much different in the 1800s, when the sport was invented. Long before there were pro teams in southern California, Texas, and Florida—and even a few years before the game moved indoors—the rules were much different than they are now.

The object of hockey was the same: Score goals by shooting a small, flat puck into your opponent's net while trying to stop the opposing team from doing the same. But in the late 1800s, it was not the high-flying, hard-hitting, wide-open game we watch today. Back then players were not allowed to pass the puck forward. Lifting the puck off the ice while taking a shot on goal was illegal too.

But hockey is an ever-evolving game. The rules have been tweaked since the first player got slashed across the wrists. Eventually the game opened up, and players were allowed to pass the puck forward. First they could make such a pass only within one of the three zones. Later they were able to pass from the defensive zone to the neutral zone. The only offside rule remaining is when an attacking player crosses the blue line and into the offensive zone before the puck.

The rule about not lifting the puck when trying to shoot a goal was dismissed too. That's why goalies started wearing big pads, giant gloves, and facemasks.

THE RINK

The game of hockey was first played on the frozen lakes and ponds of Canada and the northern United States. When it comes to the NHL, the game is played in arenas and stadiums that hold as many as 20,000 fans. In most cases, the ice surface is 200 feet (61 meters) long and 85 feet (26 m) wide. Boards about 4 feet (1.2 m) high surround the ice to keep the puck in play. Safety glass is placed on top of the boards to protect the spectators from pucks. The rink is divided into three zones, two offensive/defensive zones and the neutral zone.

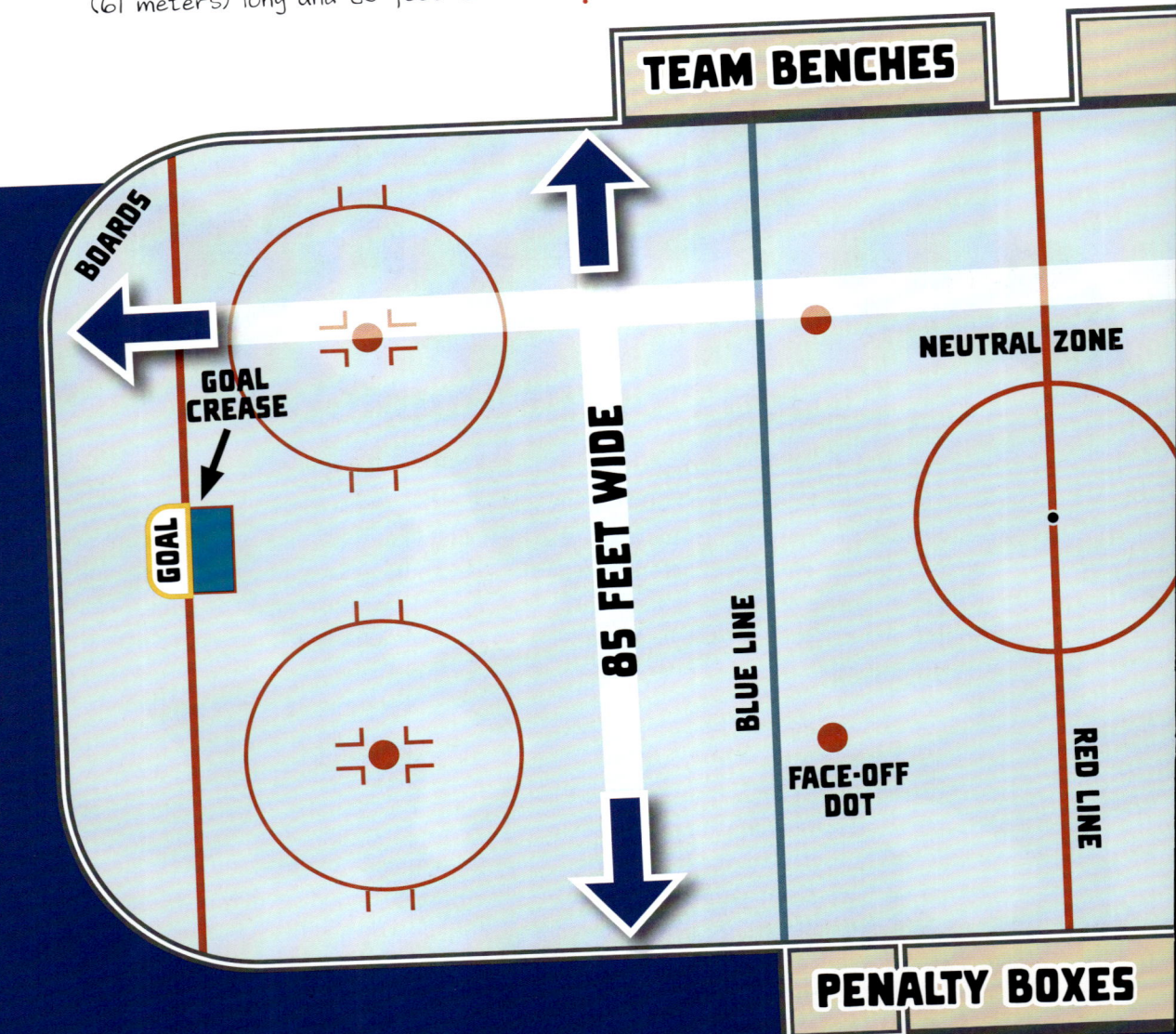

OTHER RINKS

International hockey, such as in the Olympics, is played on ice surfaces larger than NHL rinks. Olympic ice is 200 feet (61 m) long and 100 feet (30 m) wide. Many college teams in the United States also play on international-sized ice. The extra space on the rink often favors the game's better skaters.

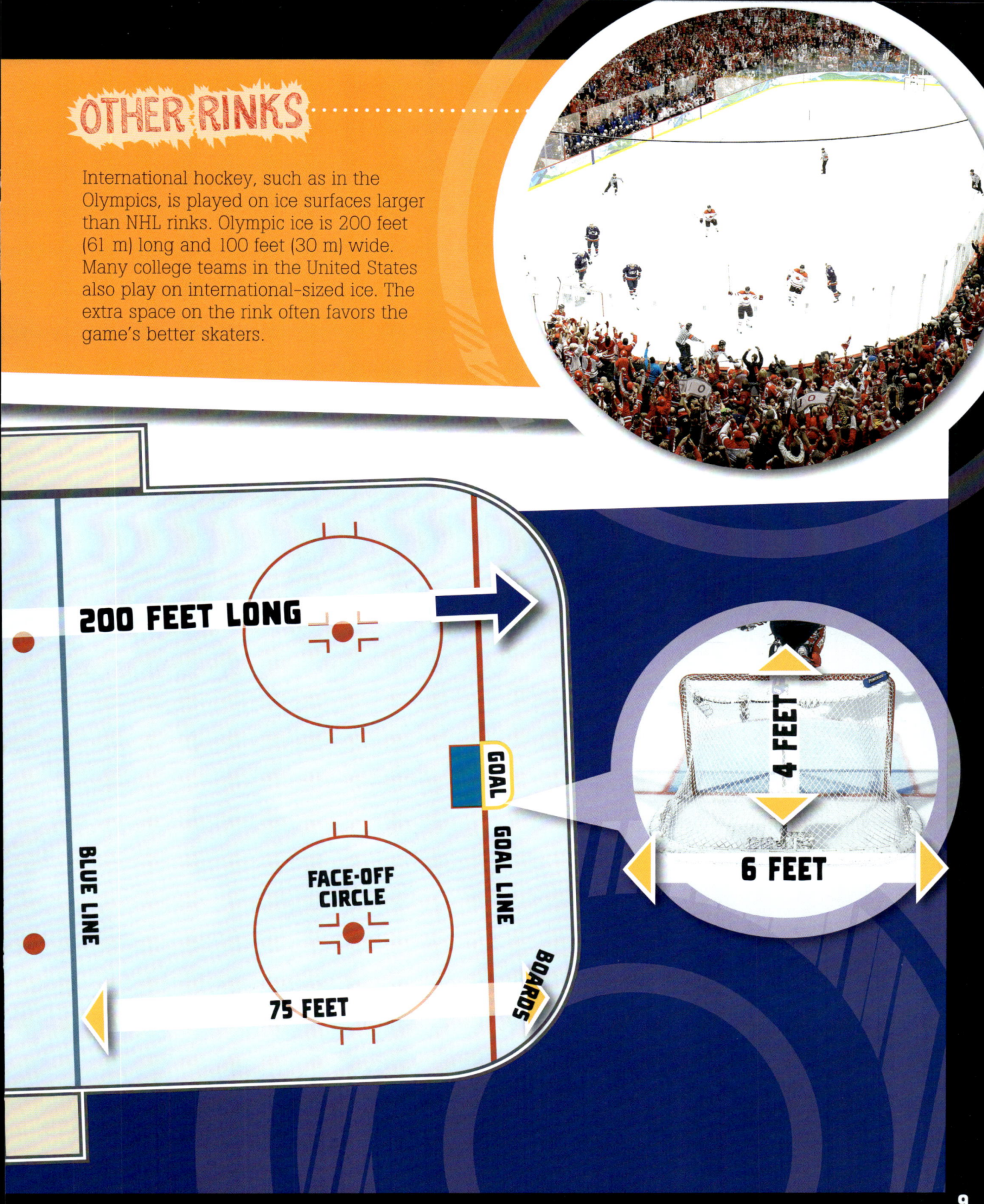

POSITIONS

When teams are playing at full strength, each team has six players on the ice: three forwards (center, left wing, right wing), two defensemen, and a goaltender.

TRIVIA

Name that Position!
Can you match the position of each of the hockey players?

1. _____
2. _____
3. _____
4. _____
5. _____
2. _____

POSITIONS
CENTER
LEFT WING
RIGHT WING
DEFENSEMAN
GOALTENDER

PENALTY PUNISHMENT

A player who commits a serious penalty, such as trying to injure another player, is immediately ejected from the game. When players are called for other penalties, such as hooking, charging, or slashing, they must leave the rink and sit in the penalty box for two, four, or five minutes. While they are in the box, their teammates must play short-handed. The short-handed team may have three or four skaters and a goalie on the ice while the other team is on the power play. Teams play short-handed until the penalty time ends or until the opponent scores a goal. Sometimes players on opposite teams get called for penalties at about the same time. Then the teams each play with four skaters and a goalie. Teams put a lot of practice into their power play and short-handed units, which are called special teams.

FACT:

If a team is down by a goal with only a few minutes remaining in the game, the coach may decide to pull the goalie off the ice. In the goalie's place, the coach can add another skater. Although it leaves the net wide open, it gives the team a 6-on-5 advantage and a better chance to score a goal.

Answer: 1. goaltender 2. defenseman 3. left wing 4. center 5. right wing

EQUIPMENT

When hockey was first played in the late 1800s, players only used a pair of skates and a stick. Over time protective gear was added, including padding and hard plastic for shins, knees, shoulders, and elbows. It took awhile for players, especially at the professional level, to get used to wearing helmets and masks.

The first NHL goalie to wear a mask was Jacques Plante. After getting his face bloodied by a puck in a 1959 game, Plante got stitched up and returned to the game with a mask. He continued to wear a mask, even though his coach didn't approve. Then more goalies started wearing masks. Andy Brown of the Pittsburgh Penguins was the last goalie to play in a game without a mask, in 1974.

In 1979 the NHL required all of the draft picks from that year forward to wear helmets. The league allowed players already in the league to play without headgear. One of the players, 1978 draft pick Craig MacTavish, played without a helmet until he retired in 1997—18 years after the helmet rule was first enforced.

In 2013 the NHL required new players to wear plastic visors for eye protection. Younger players often wear full face shields or metal cages.

JACQUES PLANTE, MONTREAL CANADIENS

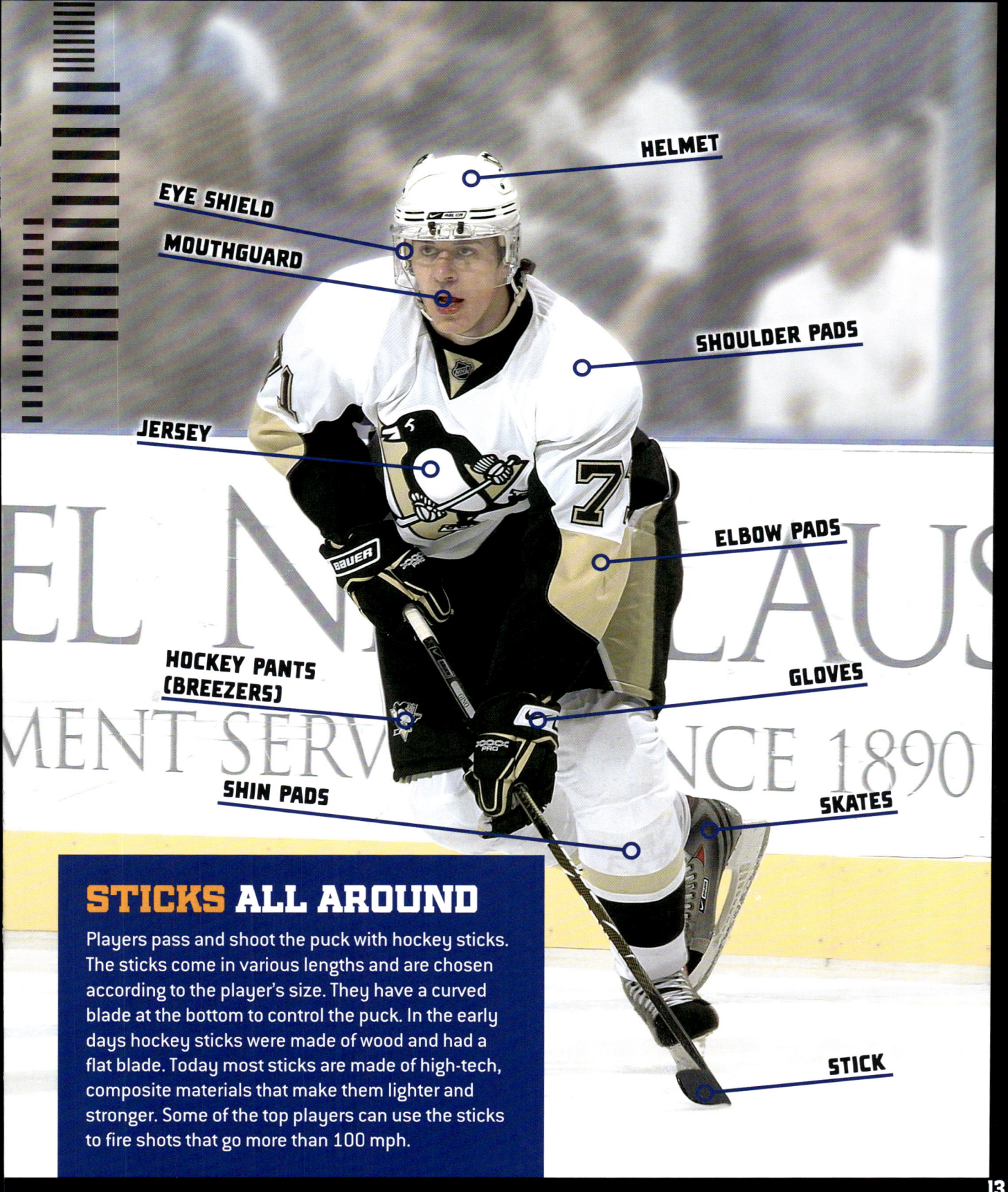

HELMET
EYE SHIELD
MOUTHGUARD
SHOULDER PADS
JERSEY
ELBOW PADS
HOCKEY PANTS (BREEZERS)
GLOVES
SHIN PADS
SKATES
STICK

STICKS ALL AROUND

Players pass and shoot the puck with hockey sticks. The sticks come in various lengths and are chosen according to the player's size. They have a curved blade at the bottom to control the puck. In the early days hockey sticks were made of wood and had a flat blade. Today most sticks are made of high-tech, composite materials that make them lighter and stronger. Some of the top players can use the sticks to fire shots that go more than 100 mph.

UNIFORMS

Football has helmets and baseball has caps, but hockey teams are defined by their jerseys. The New York Rangers have been known as the Blueshirts since their early days. The St. Louis Blues are nicknamed the "Blue Notes" because of the big, blue-winged musical note that graces the front of their jerseys.

DRESSED FOR SUCCESS

So what are the best uniforms in the NHL? Ask 30 fans and you might get 30 different answers. Here are a few that have gotten rave reviews over the years—as well as a couple that have caused critics to hold their noses. The Penguins, like Pittsburgh's other professional sports teams, wear black, yellow, and white. But originally they wore light blue sweaters. In recent years the team has occasionally brought back the powder blues. One of those times was for the Winter Classic, a pro game played in an outdoor arena.

THE GOOD

The Montreal Canadiens are one of the NHL's original teams. The team has worn similar red, white, and blue jerseys since the league started in 1917. Their "CH" logo is instantly recognizable. It stands for the team's official French name, Le Club de Hockey Canadien. (French is the official language of the Canadian province of Quebec.)

Many NHL jerseys feature several colors, but not the Detroit Red Wings' jerseys. They keep it simple and classy with red and white. The jerseys have one of the sport's most unique logos—the winged wheel—across the chest. Other teams have followed the Wings with their own feathered logos, including the Blues and the Flyers.

THE BAD

It has taken years for the Vancouver Canucks to perfect their uniforms. While their current blue, green, and white sweaters end up on best-of lists, earlier sweaters were hard on the eyes. With black, orange, and yellow as their official colors, the Canucks once sported a giant V that stretched from the player's shoulders to his belly button.

THE UGLY

Critics cried foul when the New York Islanders tried to change the jerseys that won four straight Stanley Cups. The logo featured a salty fisherman who looked like the character on a box of frozen seafood. When the Isles skated onto the ice to play their rivals—the New York Rangers—opposing fans repeatedly chanted, "We want fish sticks!" The Islanders returned to their classic jerseys in 1984 after one season.

KEEPING WARM

Do you know why hockey jerseys are sometimes called sweaters? The first hockey teams wore warm, wool, knitted sweaters when they played on outdoor ice rinks in the middle of cold winters. As games moved into indoor rinks, players wanted jerseys made out of lighter materials.

CHAPTER 2
SKATER RECORDS

Wayne Gretzky doesn't own all of the NHL's individual records. It just seems that way. "The Great One" not only broke Gordie Howe's goal-scoring record. He also shattered his hero's points mark, finishing his career with 2,857 goals and assists combined. In fact, if you took away Gretzky's goals, his career assist total would still be enough to be the NHL's all-time points leader!

It seems likely that Gretzky's points record will never be broken. Mark Messier, Gretzky's former Edmonton Oilers teammate, has come closest. Messier finished his career with 1,887 points, but that's almost 1,000 points less than Gretzky.

When it comes to individual players, records can define their greatness, whether it's over a career, a season, or even one game.

If Gretzky's scoring records won't fall, what will? Perhaps it will be Jaromir Jagr's game-winning goals record of 124. What about Ray Bourque's record for goals by a defenseman? Or Tim Kerr's single-season record for power-play goals?

▼ Wayne Gretzky

SCORING

POINTS

CAREER

1.	Wayne Gretzky	2,857	Oilers/Kings/Blues/Rangers	1979–1999
2.	Mark Messier	1,887	Oilers/Rangers/Canucks	1979–2004
3.	Gordie Howe	1,850	Red Wings/Whalers	1946–1971, 1979–1980
4.	Ron Francis	1,798	Whalers/Pens/Hurricanes/Maple Leafs	1981–2004
5.	Marcel Dionne	1,771	Red Wings/Kings/Rangers	1971–1989
6.	Steve Yzerman	1,755	Red Wings	1983–2006
7.	Jaromir Jagr	1,755	Penguins/Capitals/Rangers/Flyers/Stars/Bruins/Devils	1990–2004, 2005–2008, 2011–2014*
8.	Mario Lemieux	1,723	Penguins	1984–1994, 1995–1997, 2000–2006
9.	Joe Sakic	1,641	Nordiques/Avalanche	1988–2009
10.	Phil Esposito	1,590	Blackhawks/Bruins/Rangers	1963–1981

*Active player

▼ Mark Messier

▼ Gordie Howe

WORLD HOCKEY ASSOCIATION

Wayne Gretzky also scored 110 points (46 goals, 64 assists) in the World Hockey Association. He played one year in the WHA before the Oilers merged into the NHL. Gordie Howe played six seasons in the WHA after a long career with the Red Wings and scored 508 points (174 goals, 334 assists) in that league.

POINTS

▼ Mario Lemieux

SINGLE SEASON

1.	Wayne Gretzky	215	Oilers	1985–86
2.	Wayne Gretzky	212	Oilers	1981–82
3.	Wayne Gretzky	208	Oilers	1984–85
4.	Wayne Gretzky	205	Oilers	1983–84
5.	Mario Lemieux	199	Penguins	1988–89
6.	Wayne Gretzky	196	Oilers	1982–83
7.	Wayne Gretzky	183	Oilers	1986–87
8.	Mario Lemieux	168	Penguins	1987–88
	Wayne Gretzky	168	Kings	1988–89
10.	Wayne Gretzky	164	Oilers	1980–81

POINTS ALL AROUND

Darryl Sittler of the Toronto Maple Leafs compiled 10 points in a single game in 1976. He scored six goals and assisted on four others in an 11-4 victory over the Boston Bruins. On 16 occasions players have recorded eight-point games. Mario Lemieux did it three times, and Wayne Gretzky did it twice. The record for points in a period is six, set by the New York Islanders' Bryan Trottier in 1978.

▼ Bryan Trottier

RECORD FACT Joe Malone scored seven goals in a game in 1920 for the Quebec Bulldogs. Seven players have scored six goals in a game, including Malone that same season. Eleven players have scored four goals in one period of play.

GOALS

CAREER

1.	Wayne Gretzky	894	Oilers/Kings/Blues/Rangers	1979–1999
2.	Gordie Howe	801	Red Wings/Whalers	1946–1971, 1979–1980
3.	Brett Hull	741	Flames/Blues/Stars/Red Wings/Coyotes	1986–2006
4.	Marcel Dionne	731	Red Wings/Kings/Rangers	1971–1989
5.	Phil Esposito	717	Blackhawks/Bruins/Rangers	1963–1981
6.	Mike Gartner	708	Capitals/North Stars/Rangers/Maple Leafs/Coyotes	1979–1998
7.	Jaromir Jagr	681	Penguins/Capitals/Rangers/Flyers/Stars/Bruins/Devils	1990–2004, 2005–2008, 2011–2014*
8.	Mark Messier	694	Oilers/Rangers/Canucks	1979–2004
9.	Steve Yzerman	692	Red Wings	1983–2006
10.	Mario Lemieux	690	Penguins	1984–1994, 1995–1997, 2000–2006

*Active player

▼ Brett Hull

SINGLE SEASON

1.	Wayne Gretzky	92	Oilers	1981–82
2.	Wayne Gretzky	87	Oilers	1983–84
3.	Brett Hull	86	Blues	1990–91
4.	Mario Lemieux	85	Penguins	1988–89
5.	Phil Esposito	76	Bruins	1970–71
	Alexander Mogilny	76	Sabres	1992–93
	Teemu Selanne	76	Jets	1992–93
8.	Wayne Gretzky	73	Oilers	1984–85
9.	Brett Hull	72	Blues	1989–90
10.	Wayne Gretzky	71	Oilers	1982–83
	Jari Kurri	71	Oilers	1984–85

▲ Alexander Mogilny

POWER-PLAY GOALS

CAREER

#	Player	Goals	Teams	Years
1.	Dave Andreychuk	274	Sabres/Maple Leafs/Devils/Bruins/Avalanche/Lightning	1982–2006
2.	Brett Hull	265	Flames/Blues/Stars/Red Wings/Coyotes	1986–2006
3.	Teemu Selanne	255	Jets/Ducks/Sharks/Avalanche	1992–2014
4.	Phil Esposito	249	Blackhawks/Bruins/Rangers	1963–1981
5.	Luc Robitaille	247	Kings/Penguins/Rangers/Red Wings	1986–2006
6.	Brendan Shanahan	237	Devils/Blues/Whalers/Red Wings/Rangers	1987–2009
7.	Mario Lemieux	236	Penguins	1984–1994, 1995–1997, 2000–2006
8.	Marcel Dionne	234	Red Wings/Kings/Rangers	1971–1989
9.	Dino Ciccarelli	232	North Stars/Capitals/Red Wings/Lightning/Panthers	1980–1999
10.	Mike Gartner	217	Capitals/North Stars/Rangers/Maple Leafs/Coyotes	1979–1998

▼ Dave Andreychuk

SINGLE SEASON

#	Player	Goals	Team	Year
1.	Tim Kerr	34	Flyers	1985–86
2.	Dave Andreychuk	32	Sabres/Maple Leafs	1992–93
3.	Mario Lemieux	31	Penguins	1988–89
	Mario Lemieux	31	Penguins	1995–96
	Joe Nieuwendyk	31	Flames	1987–88
6.	Michel Goulet	29	Nordiques	1987–88
	Brett Hull	29	Blues	1990–91
	Brett Hull	29	Blues	1992–93
9.	Four players tied with	28		

▲ Tim Kerr

SHORT-HANDED GOALS

▼ Steve Yzerman

CAREER

1.	Wayne Gretzky	73	Oilers/Kings/Blues/Rangers	1979–1999
2.	Mark Messier	63	Oilers/Rangers/Canucks	1979–2004
3.	Steve Yzerman	50	Red Wings	1983–2006
4.	Mario Lemieux	49	Penguins	1984–1994, 1995–1997, 2000–2006
5.	Butch Goring	40	Kings/Islanders/Bruins	1969–1985
6.	Dave Poulin	39	Flyers/Bruins/Capitals	1982–1995
7.	Jari Kurri	37	Oilers/Kings/Rangers/Ducks/Avalanche	1980–1990, 1991–1998
8.	Sergei Fedorov	36	Red Wings/Ducks/Blue Jackets/Capitals	1990–2009
9.	Theoren Fleury	35	Flames/Avalanche/Rangers/Blackhawks	1988–2003
	Dirk Graham	35	North Stars/Blackhawks	1983–1995

SHORT-HANDED GOALS

A team is short-handed when one of its players is in the penalty box and the other team is on a power play. Despite having fewer players, the short-handed team still has the opportunity to score. Theoren Fleury of the Calgary Flames holds the record for short-handed goals in a single game. He scored three goals on the opponents' power plays in a game in 1991.

▼ Theoren Fleury

SHORT-HANDED GOALS

▼ Brian Rolston

SINGLE SEASON

1.	Mario Lemieux	13	Penguins	1988–89
2.	Wayne Gretzky	12	Oilers	1983–84
3.	Wayne Gretzky	11	Oilers	1984–85
4.	Marcel Dionne	10	Red Wings	1974–75
	Dirk Graham	10	Blackhawks	1988–89
	Mario Lemieux	10	Penguins	1987–88
7.	Paul Coffey	9	Oilers	1985–86
	Kent Nilsson	9	Flames	1983–84
	Brian Rolston	9	Bruins	2001–02
10.	Many players tied with	8		

OVERTIME GOALS

CAREER

1.	Jaromir Jagr	18	Penguins/Capitals/Rangers/Flyers/Stars/Bruins/Devils	1990–2004, 2005–2008, 2011–2014*
2.	Patrik Elias	16	Devils	1995–2014*
3.	Sergei Fedorov	15	Red Wings/Ducks/Blue Jackets/Capitals	1990–2009
	Mats Sundin	15	Nordiques/Maple Leafs/Canucks	1990–2009
	Alex Ovechkin	15	Capitals	2005–2014*
6.	Ilya Kovalchuk	14	Thrashers/Devils	2001–2013
7.	Scott Niedermayer	13	Devils/Ducks	1991–2010
	Olli Jokinen	13	Kings/Islanders/Panthers/Coyotes/Flames/Rangers/Jets	1997–2014*
9.	Brett Hull	12	Flames/Blues/Stars/Red Wings/Coyotes	1986-2006
	Brendan Shanahan	12	Devils/Blues/Whalers/Red Wings/Rangers	1987–2009

*Active player

RECORD FACT Joe Malone of the Montreal Canadiens scored 44 goals in 20 games in 1917–18. He holds the record for the best season average of 2.2 goals per game. Wayne Gretzky holds the NHL record for points per game for a season. In 1983–84 he had 205 points in 74 games, a 2.77 average.

GAME-WINNING GOALS

▼ Jaromir Jagr

CAREER

#	Player	Goals	Teams	Years
1.	Jaromir Jagr	124	Penguins/Capitals/Rangers/Flyers/Stars/Bruins/Devils	1990–2004, 2005–2008, 2011–2014*
2.	Phil Esposito	118	Blackhawks/Bruins/Rangers	1963–1981
3.	Brett Hull	110	Flames/Blues/Stars/Red Wings/Coyotes	1986–2006
	Teemu Selanne	110	Jets/Ducks/Sharks/Avalanche	1992–2014*
5.	Brendan Shanahan	109	Devils/Blues/Whalers/Red Wings/Rangers	1987–2009
6.	Guy Lafleur	97	Canadiens/Rangers/Nordiques	1971–1985, 1988–1991
7.	Mats Sundin	96	Nordiques/Maple Leafs/Canucks	1990–2009
8.	Steve Yzerman	94	Red Wings	1983–2006
9.	Sergei Fedorov	93	Red Wings/Ducks/Blue Jackets/Capitals	1990–2009
	Joe Nieuwendyk	93	Flames/Stars/Devils/Maple Leafs/Panthers	1986–2007

*Active player

SINGLE SEASON

#	Player	Goals	Team	Year
1.	Phil Esposito	16	Bruins	1970–71
	Phil Esposito	16	Bruins	1971–72
	Michel Goulet	16	Nordiques	1983–84
4.	Pavel Bure	14	Panthers	1999–00
5.	Peter Bondra	13	Capitals	1997–98
	Jari Kurri	13	Oilers	1984–85
	Cam Neely	13	Bruins	1993–94
	Jeremy Roenick	13	Blackhawks	1991–92
9.	Many players tied with	12		

▲ Pavel Bure

 # PENALTY SHOT GOALS

▼ Mats Sundin

CAREER

1.	Pavel Bure	7	Canucks/Panthers/Rangers	1991–2003
2.	Mario Lemieux	6	Penguins	1984–1994, 1995–1997, 2000–2006
3.	Vincent Lecavalier	5	Lightning	1998–2014*
4.	Joe Sakic	4	Nordiques/Avalanche	1988–2009
	Mats Sundin	4	Nordiques/Maple Leafs/Canucks	1990–2009
	David Vyborny	4	Blue Jackets	2000–2008

*Active player

 # HAT TRICKS

CAREER

1.	Wayne Gretzky	50	Oilers/Kings/Blues/Rangers	1979–1999
2.	Mario Lemieux	40	Penguins	1984–1994 1995–1997, 2000–2006
3.	Mike Bossy	39	Islanders	1977–1987
4.	Brett Hull	33	Flames/Blues/Stars/Red Wings/Coyotes	1986–2006
5.	Phil Esposito	32	Blackhawks/Bruins/Rangers	1963–1981
6.	Marcel Dionne	28	Red Wings/Kings/Rangers	1971–1989
	Bobby Hull	28	Blackhawks/Jets/Whalers	1957–1980
8.	Maurice Richard	26	Canadiens	1942–1960
9.	Cy Denneny	25	Senators/Bruins	1917–1929
10.	Jari Kurri	23	Oilers/Kings/Rangers/Ducks/Avalanche	1980–1990, 1991–1998

▲ Mike Bossy

RECORD FACT A player can earn a hat trick by scoring three goals in a single game. Wayne Gretzky has the single-season record for hat tricks in a season with 10. In fact, he racked up 10 hat tricks in a season twice! Mario Lemieux and Mike Bossy each had a nine-hat-trick season.

POINTS IN A ROOKIE SEASON

▼ Sidney Crosby

ROOKIE SEASON				
1.	Teemu Selanne	132	Jets	1992–93
2.	Peter Stastny	109	Nordiques	1980–81
3.	Alex Ovechkin	106	Capitals	2005–06
4.	Dale Hawerchuk	103	Jets	1981–82
5.	Sidney Crosby	102	Penguins	2005–06
	Joe Juneau	102	Bruins	1992–93
7.	Mario Lemieux	100	Penguins	1984–85
8.	Neal Broten	98	North Stars	1981–82
9.	Bryan Trottier	95	Islanders	1975–76
10.	Joe Nieuwendyk	92	Flames	1987–88
	Barry Pederson	92	Bruins	1981–82

GOALS IN A ROOKIE SEASON

▲ Alex Ovechkin

ROOKIE SEASON				
1.	Teemu Selanne	76	Jets	1992–93
2.	Mike Bossy	53	Islanders	1977–78
3.	Alex Ovechkin	52	Capitals	2005–06
4.	Joe Nieuwendyk	51	Flames	1987–88
5.	Dale Hawerchuk	45	Jets	1981–82
	Luc Robitaille	45	Kings	1986–87
7.	Rick Martin	44	Sabres	1971–72
	Barry Pederson	44	Bruins	1981–82
9.	Steve Larmer	43	Blackhawks	1982–83
	Mario Lemieux	43	Penguins	1984–85

ASSISTS

▼ Ron Francis

CAREER

1.	Wayne Gretzky	1,963	Oilers/Kings/Blues/Rangers	1979–1999
2.	Ron Francis	1,249	Whalers/Penguins/Hurricanes/Maple Leafs	1981–2004
3.	Mark Messier	1,193	Oilers/Rangers/Canucks	1979–2004
4.	Ray Bourque	1,169	Bruins/Avalanche	1979–2001
5.	Paul Coffey	1,135	Oilers/Penguins/Kings/Red Wings/Whalers/Flyers/Blackhawks/Hurricanes/Bruins	1980–2001
6.	Adam Oates	1,079	Red Wings/Blues/Bruins/Capitals/Flyers/Ducks/Oilers	1985–2004
7.	Steve Yzerman	1,063	Red Wings	1983–2006
8.	Jaromir Jagr	1,050	Penguins/Capitals/Rangers/Flyers/Stars/Bruins/Devils	1990–2004 2005–2008 2011–2014
9.	Gordie Howe	1,049	Red Wings/Whalers	1946–1971, 1979–1980
10.	Marcel Dionne	1,040	Red Wings/Kings/Rangers	1971–1989

RECORD FACT Goal scorers don't get all of the glory. Each time a puck goes into the net, official scorers can award up to two assists to the passers who set up the goal. When it comes to the scoring charts, an assist is worth one point, the same as a goal.

ASSISTS

▼ Wayne Gretzky

SINGLE SEASON				
1.	Wayne Gretzky	163	Oilers	1985–86
2.	Wayne Gretzky	135	Oilers	1984–85
3.	Wayne Gretzky	125	Oilers	1982–83
4.	Wayne Gretzky	122	Kings	1990–91
5.	Wayne Gretzky	121	Oilers	1986–87
6.	Wayne Gretzky	120	Oilers	1981–82
7.	Wayne Gretzky	118	Oilers	1983–84
8.	Wayne Gretzky	114	Kings	1988–89
	Mario Lemieux	114	Penguins	1988–89
10.	Wayne Gretzky	109	Oilers	1987–88
	Wayne Gretzky	109	Oilers	1980–81

ASSIST MANIA

Wayne Gretzky holds the record for most assists in one game. Three times in his career with Edmonton—in 1980, 1985, and 1986—he assisted on seven goals in a game. The only other player to have seven assists in a game was Billy Taylor of the Detroit Red Wings in 1947. The record for most assists in a single period is five set by the Winnipeg Jets' Dale Hawerchuk in 1984.

▼ Dale Hawerchuk

RECORD FACT Mark Messier assisted on more overtime goals than any other player, helping out on 18 over his career. Messier also scored eight overtime winners, giving him a record 26 overtime points for his 25 seasons.

POINTS BY A DEFENSEMAN

CAREER

#	Player	Points	Teams	Years
1.	Ray Bourque	1,579	Bruins/Avalanche	1979–2001
2.	Paul Coffey	1,531	Oilers/Penguins/Kings/Red Wings/Whalers/Flyers/Blackhawks/Hurricanes/Bruins	1980–2001
3.	Al MacInnis	1,274	Flames/Blues	1981–2004
4.	Phil Housley	1,232	Sabres/Jets/Blues/Flames/Devils/Capitals/Blackhawks/Maple Leafs	1982–2003
5.	Larry Murphy	1,216	Kings/Capitals/North Stars/Penguins/Maple Leafs/Red Wings	1980–2001
6.	Nicklas Lidstrom	1,142	Red Wings	1991–2012
7.	Denis Potvin	1,052	Islanders	1973–1988
8.	Brian Leetch	1,028	Rangers/Maple Leafs/Bruins	1987–2006
9.	Larry Robinson	958	Canadiens/Kings	1972–1992
10.	Chris Chelios	948	Canadiens/Blackhawks/Red Wings/Thrashers	1983–2010

SINGLE SEASON

#	Player	Points	Team	Year
1.	Bobby Orr	139	Bruins	1970–71
2.	Paul Coffey	138	Oilers	1985–86
3.	Bobby Orr	135	Bruins	1974–75
4.	Paul Coffey	126	Oilers	1983–84
5.	Bobby Orr	122	Bruins	1973–74
6.	Paul Coffey	121	Oilers	1984–85
7.	Bobby Orr	120	Bruins	1969–70
8.	Bobby Orr	117	Bruins	1971–72
9.	Paul Coffey	113	Penguins	1988–89
10.	Paul Coffey	103	Penguins	1989–90
	Al MacInnis	103	Flames	1990–91

▲ Raymond Bourque

RECORD FACT Defenseman Ray Bourque holds the record for the most shots on goal for a career. During his 21 seasons, the Boston Bruins star put 6,206 shots on net.

GOALS BY A DEFENSEMAN

CAREER

#	Player	Goals	Teams	Years
1.	Ray Bourque	410	Bruins/Avalanche	1979–2001
2.	Paul Coffey	396	Oilers/Penguins/Kings/Red Wings/Whalers/Flyers/Blackhawks/Hurricanes/Bruins	1980–2001
3.	Al MacInnis	340	Flames/Blues	1981–2004
4.	Phil Housley	338	Sabres/Jets/Blues/Flames/Devils/Capitals/Blackhawks/Maple Leafs	1982–2003
5.	Denis Potvin	310	Islanders	1973–1988
6.	Larry Murphy	287	Kings/Capitals/North Stars/Penguins/Maple Leafs/ Red Wings	1980–2001
7.	Red Kelly	281	Red Wings/Maple Leafs	1947–1967
8.	Bobby Orr	270	Bruins/Blackhawks	1966–1979
9.	Nicklas Lidstrom	264	Red Wings	1991–2012
10.	Brian Leetch	247	Rangers/Maple Leafs/Bruins	1987–2006

SINGLE SEASON

#	Player	Goals	Team	Season
1.	Paul Coffey	48	Oilers	1985–86
2.	Bobby Orr	46	Bruins	1974–75
3.	Paul Coffey	40	Oilers	1983–84
4.	Doug Wilson	39	Blackhawks	1981–82
5.	Paul Coffey	37	Oilers	1984–85
	Bobby Orr	37	Bruins	1970–71
	Bobby Orr	37	Bruins	1971–72
8.	Kevin Hatcher	34	Capitals	1992–93
9.	Bobby Orr	33	Bruins	1969–70
10.	Bobby Orr	32	Bruins	1973–74

▲ Denis Potvin

RECORD FACT Ian Turnbull of the Toronto Maple Leafs is the only defenseman in NHL history to score five goals in a game. He accomplished the feat in 1977. Eight defensemen have had four-goal games, including Turnbull in 1981.

ASSISTS BY A DEFENSEMAN

CAREER

#	Player	Assists	Teams	Years
1.	Ray Bourque	1,169	Bruins/Avalanche	1979–2001
2.	Paul Coffey	1,135	Oilers/Penguins/Kings/Red Wings/Whalers/Flyers/Blackhawks/Hurricanes/Bruins	1980–2001
3.	Al MacInnis	934	Flames/Blues	1981–2004
4.	Larry Murphy	929	Kings/Capitals/North Stars/Penguins/Maple Leafs/ Red Wings	1980–2001
5.	Phil Housley	894	Sabres/Jets/Blues/Flames/Devils/Capitals/Blackhawks/Maple Leafs	1982–2003
6.	Nicklas Lidstrom	878	Red Wings	1991–2012
7.	Brian Leetch	781	Rangers/Maple Leafs/Bruins	1987–2006
8.	Chris Chelios	763	Canadiens/Blackhawks/Red Wings/Thrashers	1983–2010
9.	Larry Robinson	750	Canadiens/Kings	1972–1992
10.	Denis Potvin	742	Islanders	1973–1988

SINGLE SEASON

#	Player	Assists	Team	Season
1.	Bobby Orr	102	Bruins	1970–71
2.	Paul Coffey	90	Oilers	1985–86
	Bobby Orr	90	Bruins	1973–74
4.	Bobby Orr	89	Bruins	1974–75
5.	Bobby Orr	87	Bruins	1969–70
6.	Paul Coffey	86	Oilers	1983–84
7.	Paul Coffey	84	Oilers	1984–85
8.	Paul Coffey	83	Penguins	1988–89
9.	Brian Leetch	80	Rangers	1991–92
	Bobby Orr	80	Bruins	1971–72

▲ Bobby Orr

RECORD FACT Six defensemen have six assists in a game. The list includes hockey legends Bobby Orr and Paul Coffey. The other four players are Babe Pratt, Pat Stapleton, Ron Stackhouse, and Gary Suter.

PLUS/MINUS

A player's plus/minus record shows how the team performed while the player was on the ice. The player earns a point if his team scores a goal at even strength or short-handed, and he loses a point if the other team scores a goal. However, power play goals and penalty shots are not included in the calculation. So, for example, a player is on the ice when his team scores a regular goal (+1) and a power play goal (no change), but the other team scores two goals (-2). The player's plus/minus would be -1.

▲ Patrice Bergeron led the NHL with a +36 during the 2011–12 season.

 PLUS/MINUS

CAREER

1.	Larry Robinson	+730	Canadiens/Kings	1972–1992
2.	Bobby Orr	+597	Bruins/Blackhawks	1966–1979
3.	Ray Bourque	+528	Bruins/Avalanche	1979–2001
4.	Wayne Gretzky	+518	Oilers/Kings/Blues/Rangers	1979–1999
5.	Bobby Clarke	+506	Flyers	1969–1984
6.	Denis Potvin	+460	Islanders	1973–1988
7.	Serge Savard	+460	Canadiens/Jets	1966–1983
8.	Guy Lafleur	+453	Canadiens/Rangers/Nordiques	1971–1985, 1988–1991
9.	Bryan Trottier	+452	Islanders/Penguins	1975–1992, 1993–1994
10.	Nicklas Lidstrom	+450	Red Wings	1991–2012

▲ Bobby Clarke

PLUS/MINUS

▼ Guy Lafleur

SINGLE SEASON

1.	Bobby Orr	+124	Bruins	1970–71
2.	Larry Robinson	+120	Canadiens	1976–77
3.	Wayne Gretzky	+98	Oilers	1984–85
4.	Dallas Smith	+94	Bruins	1970–71
5.	Guy Lafleur	+89	Canadiens	1976–77
6.	Steve Shutt	+88	Canadiens	1976–77
7.	Bobby Orr	+86	Bruins	1971–72
8.	Mark Howe	+85	Flyers	1985–86
9.	Bobby Orr	+84	Bruins	1973–74
10.	Bobby Clarke	+83	Flyers	1975–76
	Brad McCrimmon	+83	Flyers	1985–86

▼ Tom Bladon

POINTS BY BLADON

Philadelphia Flyers defenseman Tom Bladon had a magical night against the Cleveland Barons in 1977. He scored four goals and assisted on four others. His eight-point game remains the highest-scoring game by an NHL defenseman, equaled later by Paul Coffey of the Edmonton Oilers. But Bladon also set a record for plus/minus that night, finishing with a +10. The Flyers won the game 11-1.

RECORD FACT Bill Mikkelson had a tough time in his four seasons in the NHL. He played in 147 career games and was –147 for his career. He holds the record for worst plus-minus in a season with –82 in 1974–75.

PENALTY MINUTES

CAREER

1.	Tiger Williams	3,966	Maple Leafs/Canucks/Red Wings/Kings/Whalers	1974–1988
2.	Dale Hunter	3,565	Nordiques/Capitals/Avalanche	1980–1999
3.	Tie Domi	3,515	Maple Leafs/Rangers/Jets	1989–2006
4.	Marty McSorley	3,381	Penguins/Oilers/Kings/Rangers/Sharks/Bruins	1983–2000
5.	Bob Probert	3,300	Red Wings/Blackhawks	1985–2002
6.	Rob Ray	3,207	Sabres/Senators	1989–2004
7.	Craig Berube	3,149	Flyers/Maple Leafs/Flames/Capitals/Islanders	1986–2003
8.	Tim Hunter	3,146	Flames/Nordiques/Canucks/Sharks	1981–1997
9.	Chris Nilan	3,043	Canadiens/Rangers/Bruins	1979–1992
10.	Rick Tocchet	2,972	Flyers/Penguins/Kings/Bruins/Capitals/Coyotes	1984–2002

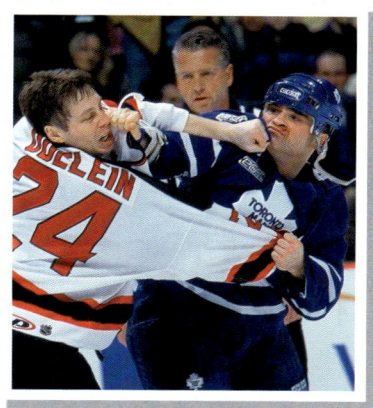

▼ Tie Domi (right) and Lyle Odelein

RECORD FACT

Penalties are measured by minutes. Minor penalties get you two minutes in the penalty box. A major penalty gets you five minutes. A misconduct is worth 10 minutes.

SINGLE SEASON

1.	Dave Schultz	472	Flyers	1974–75
2.	Paul Baxter	409	Penguins	1981–82
3.	Mike Peluso	408	Blackhawks	1991–92
4.	Dave Schultz	405	Kings/Penguins	1977–78
5.	Marty McSorley	399	Kings	1992–93
6.	Bob Probert	398	Red Wings	1987–88
7.	Basil McRae	382	North Stars	1987–88
8.	Joe Kocur	377	Red Wings	1985–86
9.	Tim Hunter	375	Flames	1988–89
10.	Donald Brashear	372	Canucks	1997–98

▲ Dave Schultz

ROUGH AND TOUGH

Chris Nilan of the Boston Bruins became the "toughest" player in the NHL on March 31, 1991. The man with the nickname "Knuckles" was penalized a record 10 times for 42 minutes during the game. He was called for six minor penalties, two major penalties, a misconduct, and a game misconduct. Another NHL tough guy, the Los Angeles Kings' Randy Holt, received nine penalties for a record 67 penalty minutes during a game in 1979.

▼ Chris Nilan

MOST SEASONS

1.	Chris Chelios	26	Canadiens/Blackhawks/Red Wings/Thrashers	1983–2010
	Gordie Howe	26	Red Wings/Whalers	1946–1971, 1979–1980
3.	Mark Messier	25	Oilers/Rangers/Canucks	1979–2004
4.	Alex Delvecchio	24	Red Wings	1950–1974
	Tim Horton	24	Maple Leafs/Rangers/Penguins/Sabres	1949–1950, 1951–1974
6.	Five players tied with	23		

▲ Chris Chelios

RECORD FACT Gordie Howe holds the record for most games played with one franchise. He played in 1,687 games for the Detroit Red Wings.

GAMES PLAYED

#	Player	Games	Teams	Years
1.	Gordie Howe	1,767	Red Wings/Whalers	1946–1971, 1979–1980
2.	Mark Messier	1,756	Oilers/Rangers/Canucks	1979–2004
3.	Ron Francis	1,731	Whalers/Penguins/Hurricanes/Maple Leafs	1981–2004
4.	Mark Recchi	1,652	Penguins/Flyers/Canadiens/Hurricanes/Thrashers/Lightning/Bruins	1988–2011
5.	Chris Chelios	1,651	Canadiens/Blackhawks/Red Wings/Thrashers	1983–2010
6.	Dave Andreychuk	1,639	Sabres/Maple Leafs/Devils/Bruins/Avalanche/Lightning	1982–2006
7.	Scott Stevens	1,635	Capitals/Blues/Devils	1982–2004
8.	Larry Murphy	1,615	Kings/Capitals/North Stars/Penguins/Maple Leafs/Red Wings	1980–2001
9.	Ray Bourque	1,612	Bruins/Avalanche	1979–2001
10.	Nicklas Lidstrom	1,564	Red Wings	1991–2012

▼ Mark Recchi

RECORD FACT Mike Sillinger was a center who played from 1990 to 2009. He played for a record 12 franchises: the Red Wings, Ducks, Canucks, Flyers, Lightning, Panthers, Senators, Blue Jackets, Coyotes, Blues, Predators, and Islanders. Four players tied for second, playing with 10 teams during their careers.

CHAPTER 3
GOALTENDER RECORDS

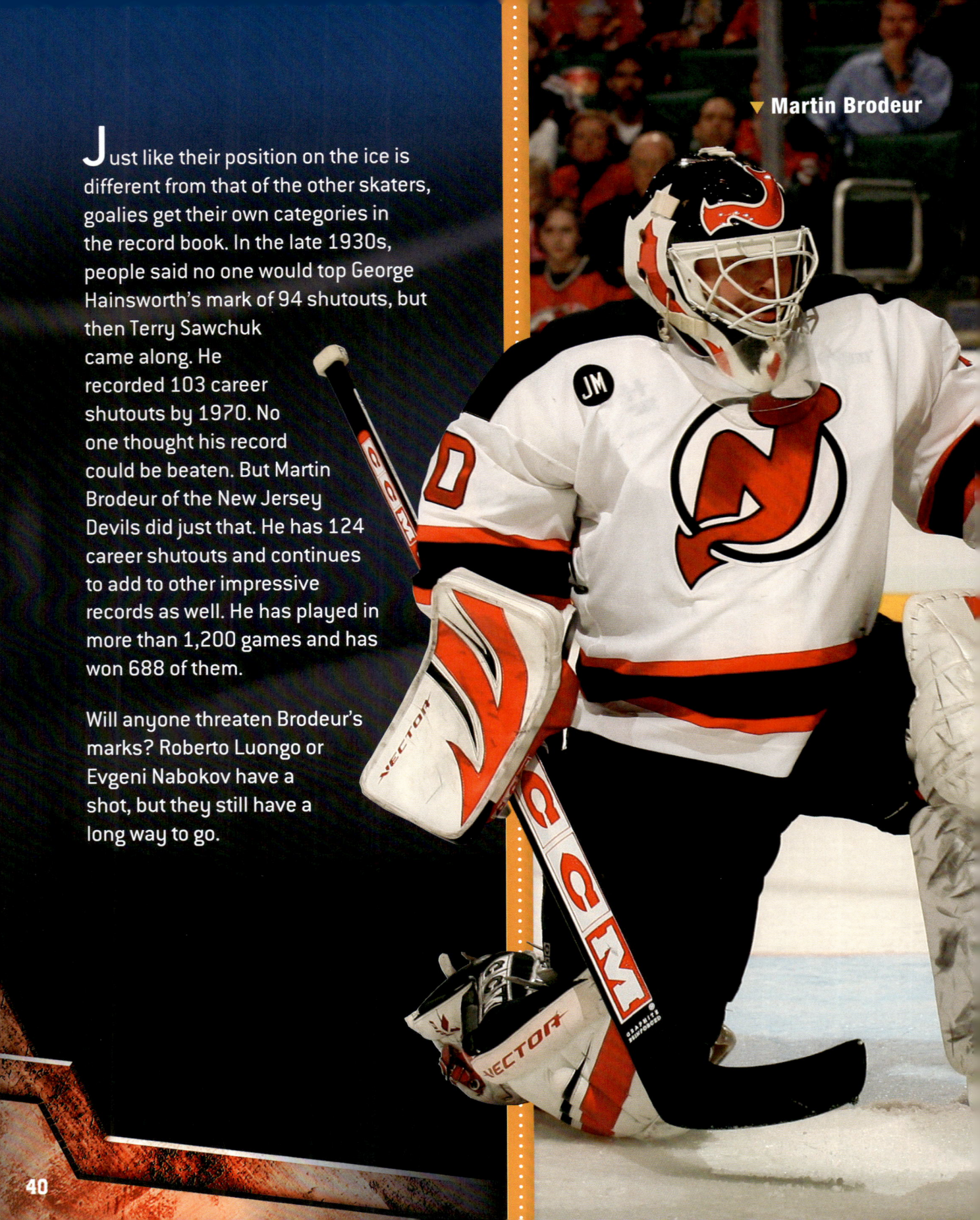

▼ Martin Brodeur

Just like their position on the ice is different from that of the other skaters, goalies get their own categories in the record book. In the late 1930s, people said no one would top George Hainsworth's mark of 94 shutouts, but then Terry Sawchuk came along. He recorded 103 career shutouts by 1970. No one thought his record could be beaten. But Martin Brodeur of the New Jersey Devils did just that. He has 124 career shutouts and continues to add to other impressive records as well. He has played in more than 1,200 games and has won 688 of them.

Will anyone threaten Brodeur's marks? Roberto Luongo or Evgeni Nabokov have a shot, but they still have a long way to go.

 # WINS

▼ Patrick Roy

CAREER

1.	Martin Brodeur	688	Devils	1991–1992, 1993–2014*
2.	Patrick Roy	551	Canadiens/Avalanche	1984–2003
3.	Ed Belfour	484	Blackhawks/Sharks/Stars/Maple Leafs/Panthers	1988–1989, 1990–2007
4.	Curtis Joseph	454	Blues/Oilers/Maple Leafs/Red Wings/Coyotes/Flames	1989–2009
5.	Terry Sawchuk	447	Red Wings/Bruins/Maple Leafs/Kings/Rangers	1949–1970
6.	Jacques Plante	437	Canadiens/Rangers/Blues/Maple Leafs/Bruins	1952–1965, 1968–1973
7.	Tony Esposito	423	Canadiens/Blackhawks	1968–1984
8.	Glenn Hall	407	Red Wings/Blackhawks/Blues	1952–1953, 1954–1971
9.	Grant Fuhr	403	Oilers/Maple Leafs/Sabres/Kings/Blues/Flames	1981–2000
10.	Chris Osgood	401	Red Wings/Islanders/Blues/	1993–2011

*Active player

RECORD FACT Martin Brodeur holds the record for career losses with 394. Goalies Gump Worsley and Curtis Joseph come in second with 352 losses each. Gary Smith of the California Golden Seals holds the record for most losses in a single season with 48 in 1970–71.

WINS

SINGLE SEASON

1.	Martin Brodeur	48	Devils	2006–07
2.	Bernie Parent	47	Flyers	1973–74
	Roberto Luongo	47	Canucks	2006–07
4.	Evgeni Nabokov	46	Sharks	2007–08
5.	Martin Brodeur	45	Devils	2009–10
	Miikka Kiprusoff	45	Flames	2008–09
7.	Martin Brodeur	44	Devils	2007–08
	Evgeni Nabokov	44	Sharks	2009–10
	Bernie Parent	44	Flyers	1974–75
	Terry Sawchuk	44	Red Wings	1950–51
	Terry Sawchuk	44	Red Wings	1951–52

▼ Roberto Luongo

KEEP ON WINNIN'

Gilles Gilbert of the Boston Bruins holds the record for consecutive victories. He won 17 straight games in 1975–76. The Bruins' Gerry Cheevers has the record for the longest undefeated streak, going 24-0-8 in 1971–72. (The NHL had ties before introducing the shootout in 2005.)

◄ Bobby Hull

▼ Gerry Cheevers

RECORD FACT Goals-against average is a stat that shows how many goals per game are allowed by the goalie on average. To find the goals-against average, take the number of goals allowed and multiply by 60. Then divide the result by the number of minutes played.

GOALS-AGAINST AVERAGE

▼ Dominik Hasek

CAREER

1.	Alec Connell	1.91	Senators/Falcons/Americans/Maroons	1924–1935, 1936–1937
2.	George Hainsworth	1.93	Canadiens/Maple Leafs	1926–1937
3.	Charlie Gardiner	2.02	Blackhawks	1927–1934
4.	Lorne Chabot	2.03	Rangers/Maple Leafs/Canadiens/Blackhawks/Maroons/Americans	1926–1937
5.	Tiny Thompson	2.08	Bruins/Red Wings	1928–1940
6.	Dave Kerr	2.15	Maroons/Americans/Rangers	1930–1941
7.	Dominik Hasek	2.20	Blackhawks/Sabres/Red Wings/Senators	1990–1995, 1996–2002, 2006–2008
8.	Martin Brodeur	2.24	Devils	1991–1992, 1993–2014*
	Ken Dryden	2.24	Canadiens	1970–1973, 1974–1979
10.	Henrik Lundqvist	2.26	Rangers	2005–2014*

*Active player

SINGLE SEASON

1.	George Hainsworth	0.92	Canadiens	1928–29
2.	George Hainsworth	1.06	Canadiens	1927–28
3.	Alec Connell	1.12	Senators	1925–26
4.	Tiny Thompson	1.15	Bruins	1928–29
5.	Roy Worters	1.16	Americans	1928–29
6.	Alec Connell	1.24	Senators	1927–28
7.	Dolly Dolson	1.38	Cougars	1928–29
8.	John Ross Roach	1.41	Rangers	1928–29
9.	Clint Benedict	1.42	Maroons	1926–27
10.	Alec Connell	1.43	Senators	1928–29

▲ Tiny Thompson

GOALS ALLOWED

CAREER

1.	Martin Brodeur	2,764	Devils	1991–1992, 1993–2014*
2.	Grant Fuhr	2,756	Oilers/Maple Leafs/Sabres/Kings/Blues/Flames	1981–2000
	Gilles Meloche	2,756	Blackhawks/Golden Seals/Barons/North Stars/Penguins	1970–1988
4.	Tony Esposito	2,563	Canadiens/Blackhawks	1968–1984
5.	Patrick Roy	2,546	Canadiens/Avalanche	1984–2003
6.	Curtis Joseph	2,516	Blues/Oilers/Maple Leafs/Red Wings/Coyotes/Flames	1989–2009
7.	John Vanbiesbrouck	2,503	Rangers/Panthers/Flyers/Islanders/Devils	1981–1982, 1983–2002
8.	Gump Worsley	2,407	Rangers/Canadiens/North Stars	1952–1953, 1954–1974
9.	Terry Sawchuk	2,389	Red Wings/Bruins/Maple Leafs/Kings/Rangers	1949–1970
10.	Tom Barrasso	2,385	Sabres/Penguins/Senators/Hurricanes/Maple Leafs/Blues	1983–2000, 2001–2003

*Active player

SINGLE SEASON

1.	Ken McAuley	310	Rangers	1943–44
2.	Greg Millen	282	Whalers	1982–83
3.	Greg Millen	258	Penguins	1980–81
4.	Gary Smith	256	Golden Seals	1970–71
5.	Craig Billington	254	Senators	1993–94
6.	Mike Liut	250	Blues	1981–82
	Peter Sidorkiewicz	250	Senators	1992–93
8.	Tony Esposito	246	Blackhawks	1980–81
	Grant Fuhr	246	Oilers	1987–88
	Harry Lumley	246	Blackhawks	1950–51

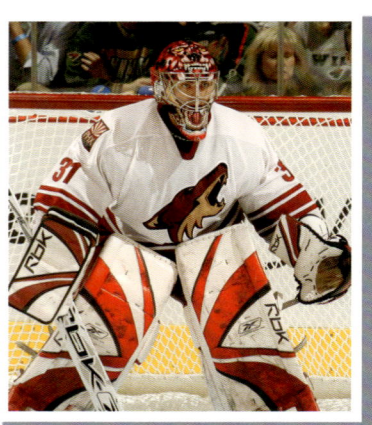

▲ Curtis Joseph

RECORD FACT

The shootout has eliminated ties from teams' and goaltenders' records. But in the pre-shootout era, Terry Sawchuck ended up with more ties than any other goaltender. He finished in a stalemate 172 times in 21 seasons.

SAVE PERCENTAGE

▼ Tim Thomas

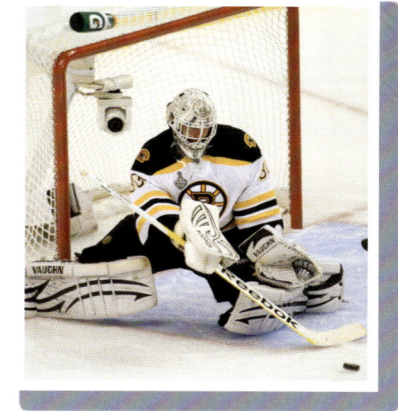

CAREER

#	Name	Pct	Teams	Years
1.	Dominik Hasek	.9223	Blackhawks/Sabres/Red Wings/Senators	1990–1995, 1996–2002, 2006–2008
2.	Henrik Lundqvist	.9025	Rangers	2005–2014*
3.	Tim Thomas	.9199	Bruins/Panthers/Stars	2002–2003, 2005–2014*
4.	Roberto Luongo	.9190	Islanders/Panthers/Canucks	1999–2014*
5.	Pekka Rinne	.9182	Predators	2005–2014*
6.	Jaroslav Halak	.9177	Canadiens/Blues/Capitals	2006–2014*
7.	Tomas Vokoun	.9169	Canadiens/Predators/Panthers/Capitals/Penguins	1996–2014*
8.	Carey Price	.9168	Canadiens	2007–2014*
9.	Jimmy Howard	.9165	Red Wings	2005–2014*
10.	Jonas Hiller	.9164	Ducks	2007–2014*

*Active player

RECORD FACT

Save percentage is a stat that shows how often a goalie stops the other team from scoring. To calculate the save percentage, divide the number of saves a goalie makes by the number of shots on goal.

SINGLE SEASON

#	Name	Pct	Team	Year
1.	Craig Anderson	.9409	Senators	2012–13
2.	Brian Elliott	.9403	Blues	2011–12
3.	Tim Thomas	.9382	Bruins	2010–11
4.	Dominik Hasek	.9366	Sabres	1998–99
5.	Corey Schneider	.9365	Canucks	2011–12
6.	Josh Harding	.9333	Wild	2013–14
7.	Miikka Kiprusoff	.9327	Flames	2003–04
	Dwayne Roloson	.9327	Wild	2003–04
	Tim Thomas	.9327	Bruins	2008–09
10.	Marty Turco	.9323	Stars	2002–03

▲ Miikka Kiprusoff

45

SAVES

CAREER

#	Player	Saves	Teams	Years
1.	Martin Brodeur	28,776	Devils	1991–1992, 1993–2014*
2.	Patrick Roy	25,807	Canadiens/Avalanche	1984–2003
3.	Curtis Joseph	24,279	Blues/Oilers/Maple Leafs/Red Wings/Coyotes/Flames	1989–2009
4.	Ed Belfour	22,434	Blackhawks/Sharks/Stars/Maple Leafs/Panthers	1988–1989, 1990–2007
5.	John Vanbiesbrouck	22,176	Rangers/Panthers/Flyers/Islanders/Devils	1981–1982, 1983–2002
6.	Roberto Luongo	21,886	Islanders/Panthers/Canucks	1999–2014*
7.	Sean Burke	21,009	Devils/Whalers/Hurricanes/Canucks/Flyers/Panthers/Coyotes/Lightning/Kings	1987–1991, 1992–2007
8.	Nikolai Khabibulin	20,258	Jets/Coyotes/Lightning/Blackhawks/Oilers	1994–1999, 2000–2014*
9.	Tom Barrasso	19,705	Sabres/Penguins/Senators/Hurricanes/Maple Leafs/Blues	1983–2000, 2001–2003
10.	Grant Fuhr	19,403	Oilers/Maple Leafs/Sabres/Kings/Blues/Flames	1981–2000

*Active player

SINGLE SEASON

#	Player	Saves	Team	Season
1.	Roberto Luongo	2,303	Panthers	2003–04
2.	Roberto Luongo	2,275	Panthers	2005–06
3.	Felix Potvin	2,214	Maple Leafs	1996–97
4.	Cam Ward	2,191	Hurricanes	2010–11
5.	Marc Denis	2,172	Blue Jackets	2002–03
6.	Curtis Joseph	2,169	Blues	1993–94
7.	Bill Ranford	2,089	Oilers	1993–94
8.	Craig Anderson	2,047	Avalanche	2009–10
9.	Tomas Vokoun	2,033	Panthers	2007–08
10.	Dominik Hasek	2,024	Sabres	1996–97

▲ Cam Ward

GOALS NOT WELCOME

Many of the NHL's shutout records were set when attacking teams were not allowed to pass the puck forward in the offensive zone. The longest shutout stretch by a goaltender lasted 461 minutes, 29 seconds. Alec Connell of the Ottawa Senators set that record in 1928 and had six consecutive shutouts along the way. In the modern era, the Phoenix Coyotes' Brian Boucher had five consecutive shutouts in 2003–04, holding opponents scoreless for 332 minutes, 1 second.

Brian Boucher

GAMES PLAYED (GOALIES)

1.	Martin Brodeur	1,259	Devils	1991–1992, 1993–2014*
2.	Patrick Roy	1,029	Canadiens/Avalanche	1984–2003
3.	Terry Sawchuk	971	Red Wings/Bruins/Maple Leafs/Kings/Rangers	1949–1970
4.	Ed Belfour	963	Blackhawks/Sharks/Stars/Maple Leafs/Panthers	1988–1989, 1990–2007
5.	Curtis Joseph	943	Blues/Oilers/Maple Leafs/Red Wings/Coyotes/Flames	1989–2009
6.	Glenn Hall	906	Red Wings/Blackhawks/Blues	1952–1953, 1954–1971
7.	Tony Esposito	886	Canadiens/Blackhawks	1968–1984
8.	John Vanbiesbrouck	882	Rangers/Panthers/Flyers/Islanders/Devils	1981–1982, 1983–2002
9.	Grant Fuhr	868	Oilers/Maple Leafs/Sabres/Kings/Blues/Flames	1981–2000
10.	Gump Worsley	861	Rangers/Canadiens/North Stars	1952–1953, 1954–1974

*Active player

SHUTOUTS

CAREER

1.	Martin Brodeur	124	Devils	1991–1992, 1993–2014*
2.	Terry Sawchuk	103	Red Wings/Bruins/Maple Leafs/Kings/Rangers	1949–1970
3.	George Hainsworth	94	Canadiens/Maple Leafs	1926–1937
4.	Glenn Hall	84	Red Wings/Blackhawks/Blues	1952–1953, 1954–1971
5.	Jacques Plante	82	Canadiens/Rangers/Blues/Maple Leafs/Bruins	1952–1965, 1968–1973
6.	Alec Connell	81	Senators/Falcons/Americans/Maroons	1924–1935, 1936–1937
	Dominik Hasek	81	Blackhawks/Sabres/Red Wings/Senators	1990–1995, 1996–2002, 2006–2008
	Tiny Thompson	81	Bruins/Red Wings	1928–1940
9.	Ed Belfour	76	Blackhawks/Sharks/Stars/Maple Leafs/Panthers	1988–1989, 1990–2007
	Tony Esposito	76	Canadiens/Blackhawks	1968–1940

*Active player

▼ Jacques Plante

SINGLE SEASON

1.	George Hainsworth	22	Canadiens	1928–29
2.	Alec Connell	15	Senators	1925–26
	Alec Connell	15	Senators	1927–28
	Tony Esposito	15	Blackhawks	1969–70
	Hal Winkler	15	Bruins	1927–28
6.	George Hainsworth	14	Canadiens	1926–27
7.	Seven players tied with	13		

GOALS FOR GOALIES

Goalies usually miss out on the glory of scoring a goal. But goalies have proven they can score too. Ten goaltenders have been credited with scoring goals. For some, they were simply the last offensive player to touch the puck before a defensive player put the puck in his own net. However, some have shot and scored into an open net. In 2013 Martin Brodeur became the first goaltender to be credited for a third goal.

▼ Martin Brodeur

▼ Jose Theodore

GOAL-SCORING GOALIES

Billy Smith	Islanders	Nov. 28, 1979
Ron Hextall	Flyers	Dec. 8, 1987
Ron Hextall	Flyers	April 11, 1989
Chris Osgood	Red Wings	March 6, 1996
Martin Brodeur	Devils	April 17, 1997
Damian Rhodes	Senators	Jan. 2, 1999
Martin Brodeur	Devils	Feb. 15, 2000
Jose Theodore	Canadiens	Jan. 2, 2001
Evgeni Nabokov	Sharks	March 10, 2002
Mika Noronen	Sabres	Feb. 14, 2004
Chris Mason	Predators	April 15, 2006
Cam Ward	Hurricanes	Dec. 26, 2011
Martin Brodeur	Devils	March 21, 2013

RECORD FACT

In 1993 the Calgary Flames defeated the San Jose Sharks 13-1. Goaltender Jeff Reese assisted on three of the goals No other goalie has had a three-point game.

Chapter 4: PLAYERS

FORWARDS

Forwards skate up front and get down deep. These right wings, left wings, and centers are the driving force behind putting points on the scoreboard. If the forwards don't start the offense, they usually finish it with nifty passes and gritty goals.

WAYNE GRETZKY

Wayne Gretzky's records will likely stand for a long time. "The Great One" was the only player to score more than 200 points in a single season—a feat he accomplished four times. His best season was 1985–1986 when he scored 52 goals and had 163 assists for 215 points. In 1981–1982 he scored a record 92 goals. For his career, Gretzky recorded 2,857 points, but his 1,963 assists alone would put him at the top of the all-time scoring list. The NHL retired Gretzky's 99 jersey number, meaning no player from any team can wear the number.

GORDIE HOWE

Gordie Howe was called Mr. Hockey for a good reason. He led the NHL in points six times, but he was also known for his rough-and-tumble play. Any player who scores a goal, gets an assist, and gets in a fight achieves a "Gordie Howe hat trick." Howe played professional hockey until 1980 at age 51. During his final three seasons, he played for the New England Whalers along with his sons, Mark and Marty. In 1997, when Howe was 69 years old, the Detroit Vipers of the International Hockey League signed him to play in one game, making Howe the first professional hockey player to play in six different decades.

MARIO LEMIEUX

Who knows how many points "Super" Mario Lemieux would have scored had he been healthy for his entire career. Still, a battle with cancer and back surgery couldn't keep the Pittsburgh star sidelined for good. Three years after retiring, being inducted into the Hall of Fame, and becoming part-owner of the Penguins, he made a comeback and played five more seasons for Pittsburgh. Lemieux is the only person in history to win a Stanley Cup as a player and as an owner.

Top Forwards

- Jean Beliveau, Canadiens—named to 13 All-Star Games
- Wayne Gretzky, Oilers/Kings/Blues/Rangers—hockey's all-time leading scorer
- Gordie Howe, Red Wings/Houston Aeros/Whalers—played 32 seasons of professional hockey
- Bobby Hull, Blackhawks/Jets/Whalers—four-time MVP (two in NHL, two in the World Hockey Association)
- Guy Lafleur, Canadiens/Rangers/Nordiques—two-time MVP
- Mario Lemieux, Penguins—won three MVP awards
- Mark Messier, Oilers/Rangers/Canucks/Indianapolis Racers/Stingers—named to 15 All-Star Games
- Stan Mikita, Blackhawks—four-time scoring leader
- Howie Morenz, Canadiens/Blackhawks/Rangers—three-time MVP
- Maurice Richard, Canadiens—led Montreal to eight Stanley Cup wins

JEAN BELIVEAU

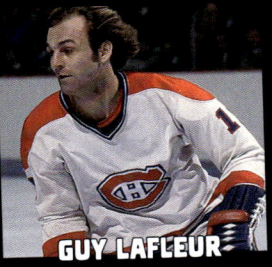
GUY LAFLEUR

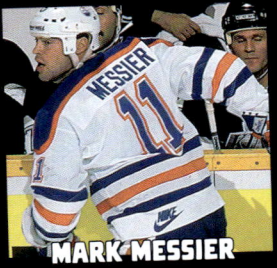
MARK MESSIER

MAURICE RICHARD

DEFENSEMEN

They're known as the blue liners and are often the last line of defense before the goaltender. But defensemen do much more than take on the other team's forwards. The best defenders can score too.

SCOTT NIEDERMAYER

BOBBY ORR

Bobby Orr changed the defenseman position forever in the NHL. There were offensive defensemen before Orr, but few could skate or handle the puck like him. During one penalty kill, he skated for 21 seconds without losing the puck before scoring a short-handed goal. He was named the NHL's MVP three times in his career.

CHRIS CHELIOS

You can't keep Chris Chelios down. After playing more than 24 seasons in the NHL, he played minor-league hockey from 2008 to 2010. Then the NHL called him one more time. In 2009–2010, at the age of 48, he played seven games for the Atlanta Thrashers before retiring in August. No defenseman has played in more NHL games than Chelios. In fact, only three other players—all forwards—have played more.

DOUG HARVEY

Doug Harvey was a big reason why the Montreal Canadiens won five Stanley Cups in a row from 1956–1960. He was a great defender who blocked shots and moved the puck out of his team's end. He also excelled on power plays and passing the puck to his high-scoring teammates. Harvey won the Norris Trophy as the NHL's best defenseman seven times. Only Bobby Orr has won the award more times.

Top Defensemen

- Ray Bourque, Bruins/Avalanche—voted to 19 All-Star Games
- Chris Chelios, Canadiens/Blackhawks/Red Wings/Thrashers—played 26 seasons in the league
- Paul Coffey, Oilers/Penguins/Kings/Red Wings/Whalers/Flyers/Blackhawks/Hurricanes/Bruins—ranks second among defensemen in career goals (396)
- Doug Harvey, Canadiens/Rangers/Red Wings/Blues—13-time All-Star Game pick
- Red Kelly, Red Wings/Maple Leafs—selected for the All-Star Game 12 times
- Nicklas Lidstrom, Red Wings—11-time All Star won the Norris Trophy seven times
- Bobby Orr, Bruins/Blackhawks—named NHL's best defenseman eight times
- Denis Potvin, Islanders—named league's best defenseman three times
- Larry Robinson, Canadiens/Kings—twice named league's best defenseman
- Eddie Shore, Bruins/New York Americans—four-time MVP

RAY BOURQUE | PAUL COFFEY | NICKLAS LIDSTROM | DENIS POTVIN

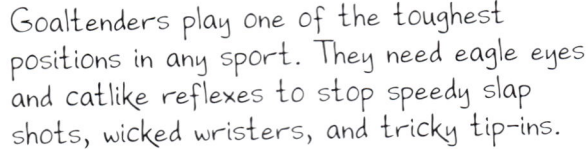
GOALTENDERS

Goaltenders play one of the toughest positions in any sport. They need eagle eyes and catlike reflexes to stop speedy slap shots, wicked wristers, and tricky tip-ins.

ROBERTO LUONGO

PATRICK ROY

You couldn't script a better full first season than the one Patrick Roy had. By the time the 1986 playoffs started during his rookie year, he was the Canadiens' number one goalie. He led the team all the way to the Stanley Cup championship. He allowed fewer than two goals per game during the playoffs and won the Conn Smythe Award as the playoff MVP. Over the next 17 seasons, "St. Patrick" won three more titles—one with Montreal and two with the Colorado Avalanche.

MARTIN BRODEUR

Patrick Roy's records seemed unbreakable when he retired in 2003, but Martin Brodeur proved he was up to the task. Drafted in 1990, he has spent his entire career with the New Jersey Devils. He has won three Stanley Cups and owns some of the game's most spectacular saves with his unique defensive style. Brodeur has more wins (688) and more shutouts (124) than any other goalie in league history.

JACQUES PLANTE

Jacques Plante's influence on the game is still felt today. He was the first NHL goaltender to regularly wear a mask to protect his face from flying pucks, although others had tried it briefly. Even though his coach didn't like the look at first, Plante kept the mask as the Canadiens won 18 games in a row. He won six Stanley Cups and was one of the few goaltenders to win the Hart Trophy as league MVP.

Top Goaltenders

- Turk Broda, Maple Leafs—led Toronto to five championships
- Martin Brodeur, Devils—owns most of the NHL's career goalie records
- Ken Dryden, Canadiens—won six Stanley Cups in eight-year career
- Bill Durnan, Canadiens—voted NHL's top goalie six times
- George Hainsworth, Canadiens/Maple Leafs—voted league's best goalie three times
- Dominik Hasek, Blackhawks/Sabres/Red Wings/Senators—only goalie to win two MVPs
- Jacques Plante, Canadiens/Rangers/Blues/Maple Leafs/Bruins/Oilers—led Montreal to five Cup wins in a row
- Patrick Roy, Canadiens/Avalanche—playoff MVP in three of his four Stanley Cup wins
- Terry Sawchuk, Red Wings/Bruins/Maple Leafs/Kings/Rangers—voted top goalie four times

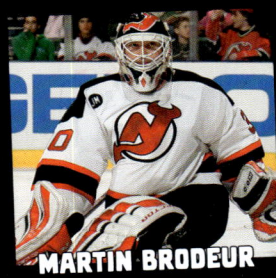
MARTIN BRODEUR

KEN DRYDEN

DOMINIK HASEK

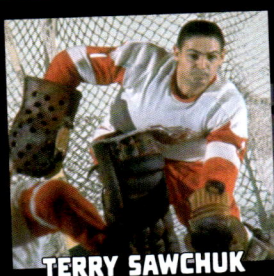
TERRY SAWCHUK

CURRENT & RISING STARS

The NHL has had a legendary past, but it also has a bright future. The league currently has several players striving for the Hall of Fame. From Joe Thornton to Sidney Crosby, these stars add an exciting spark to pro hockey.

SIDNEY CROSBY

Few players have burst onto the hockey scene like Pittsburgh Penguins star Sidney Crosby. "Sid the Kid" was only 19 years old when he was named the team captain—at the time the youngest captain in NHL history. He also became the league's youngest scoring champion and the second-youngest MVP after Wayne Gretzky. In 2014 he won the Hart trophy as MVP for the second time.

ALEX OVECHKIN

It didn't take long for Alex Ovechkin to become a superstar. In 2006 the Russian left wing won the Calder Trophy as rookie of the year. Two seasons later he was the league MVP, winning the first of three Hart Trophies. He scored 50 or more goals and more than 100 points in four of his first five seasons. In 2014, he scored his 400th goal, becoming the sixth-fastest player to reach that milestone.

HENRIK AND DANIEL SEDIN

Two of the best players in the NHL are twin brothers Henrik (left) and Daniel Sedin of the Vancouver Canucks. In 1999 the Canucks made a trade to get the second- and third-overall picks in the summer draft and took the Sedin twins. Through their first 13 seasons, Daniel has 307 goals and 805 points, and Henrik has 193 goals and 842 points. In 2010 Henrik led the NHL with 83 assists and 112 points. Not to be outdone, Daniel scored 104 points in 2011, the best in the NHL.

Top Current & Rising Stars

- Drew Doughty, D, Kings—Key figure on Los Angeles's 2012 ans 2014 championships
- Patrick Kane, F, Blackhawks—2008 rookie of the year and three-time All-Star
- Erik Karlsson, D, Senators—Top-scoring defenseman in two of his first five seasons
- Evgeni Malkin, F, Penguins—2007 rookie of the year and 2012 MVP
- Rick Nash, F, Blue Jackets/Rangers—has been selected to the All-Star Game five times
- Jonathan Quick, G, Kings—backstopped championships in 2012 and 2014
- Steven Stamkos, F, Lightning—two-time league leader in goal scoring
- P.K. Subban, D, Canadiens—named the league's best defenseman in 2013
- John Tavares, F, Islanders—NHL's first overall draft pick in 2009
- Jonathan Toews, F, Blackhawks—captained Chicago to Stanley Cup wins in 2010 and 2013

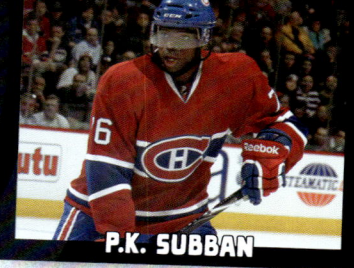
P.K. SUBBAN

EVGENI MALKIN

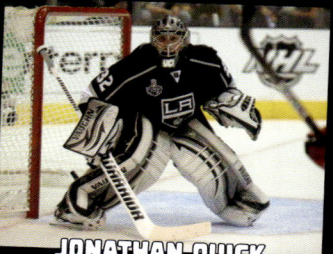
JONATHAN QUICK

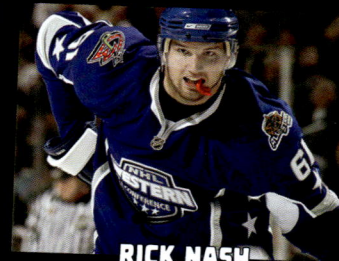
RICK NASH

MVPS

After every season the NHL awards the Hart Trophy to the season's best player. It is the league's most valuable player award, and it has gone to some great hockey stars.

TRADED AWAY

During the 2005–2006 season, the Boston Bruins sent Joe Thornton all the way across the country, trading him to the San Jose Sharks. Thornton joined a team that was 8–12–4 and had lost 10 games in a row. But he led the Sharks to a 36–15–7 record the rest of the way. Thornton was the only player in NHL history to be traded during the season in which he won the MVP.

GREATNESS HAS HART

The great Wayne Gretzky won nine Hart Trophies, including an amazing eight in a row from 1980 to 1987 with the Edmonton Oilers. In 1989, after "the trade of the century" sent Gretzky to the Kings, he won his final MVP award. Mario Lemieux broke up Gretzky's streak after a 168-point season in 1988–1989, winning the first of his three Hart Trophies.

GOALIES ARE VALUABLE TOO

Goaltenders have their own postseason awards, but they have also been voted as the MVP seven times in NHL history. The first goalie to receive the award was the New York Americans' Roy Worters in 1929. In 1997 the Sabres' Dominik Hasek became the first goalie since Jacques Plante in 1962 to be named MVP. He won the award again the following year, becoming the only goalie to win the award twice. The most recent goalie to win the award was the Canadiens' Jose Theodore in 2002.

MULTIPLE MVP WINNERS

Player	Team	Awards
Wayne Gretzky	Oilers/Kings	9
Gordie Howe	Red Wings	6
Eddie Shore	Bruins	4
Bobby Clarke	Flyers	3
Mario Lemieux	Penguins	3
Howie Morenz	Canadiens	3
Bobby Orr	Bruins	3
Alex Ovechkin	Capitals	3
Jean Beliveau	Canadiens	2
Bill Cowley	Bruins	2
Phil Esposito	Bruins	2
Dominik Hasek	Sabres	2
Bobby Hull	Blackhawks/Blues	2
Guy Lafleur	Canadiens	2
Mark Messier	Rangers/Oilers	2
Stan Mikita	Blackhawks	2
Nels Stewart	Maroons	2
Sidney Crosby	Penguins	2

DREAM TEAM

Imagine a team made up of the greatest players who ever skated onto a hockey rink. Few would argue that Wayne Gretzky should be the number one center. But from there picking the lineup would be almost impossible. Is Martin Brodeur the best goalie, or is Patrick Roy? How do you choose between Nicklas Lidstrom and Chris Chelios on defense? Is Bobby Hull the best left wing of all time? Is Brett Hull the best right wing?

Most hockey teams play with four forward lines consisting of a center, left wing, and right wing, three defensive pairs, and up to three goalies.

IF YOU WERE THE COACH, WHO WOULD YOU PICK FOR YOUR TEAM?

Left Wing

Bobby Hull, Blackhawks

Alex Ovechkin, Capitals

Luc Robitaille, Kings

Frank Mahovlich, Maple Leafs

Right Wing

Gordie Howe, Red Wings

Maurice Richard, Canadiens

Mike Bossy, Islanders

Brett Hull, Blues

Center

- Wayne Gretzky, Oilers
- Mario Lemieux, Penguins
- Mark Messier, Oilers
- Jean Beliveau, Canadiens

Goaltender

- Patrick Roy, Avalanche
- Martin Brodeur, Devils
- Terry Sawchuk, Red Wings

Defenseman

- Bobby Orr, Bruins
- Doug Harvey, Canadiens
- Ray Bourque, Bruins
- Nicklas Lidstrom, Red Wings
- Eddie Shore, Bruins
- Denis Potvin, Islanders

CURRENT VS. CLASSIC

What was the best era of the NHL? The days when only the Original Six teams existed? The rough-and-tough days of the 1970s? Are we seeing it today? Can you even compare various periods of the NHL? Look at some of today's stars matched up against some of yesterday's best. Who do you think is better?

LEFT WING

Alex Ovechkin, Capitals	Bobby Hull, Blackhawks/Jets/Whalers*
6 feet 2 inches (188 cm) 223 pounds (101 kg)	5 feet 10 inches (178 cm) 195 pounds (88 kg)
2005–present	1957–1980
422 goals 392 assists 814 points 456 penalty minutes	913 goals 895 assists 1,808 points 823 penalty minutes

RIGHT WING

Jarome Iginla, Flames/Penguins/Bruins	Gordie Howe, Red Wings/Aeros/Whalers*
6 feet 1 inch (185 cm) 207 pounds (94 kg)	6 feet (183 cm) 205 pounds (93 kg)
1996–present	1946–1980
560 goals 607 assists 1,157 points 887 penalty minutes	975 goals 1,383 assists 2,358 points 2,084 penalty minutes

JAROME IGINLA

All stats are through the 2012–13 season.

CENTER

Sidney Crosby, Penguins	Wayne Gretzky, Oilers/Kings/Blues/Rangers*
5 feet 11 inches (180 cm) 200 pounds (91 kg)	6 feet (183 cm) 185 pounds (84 kg)
2005–present	1978–1999
274 goals 495 assists 769 points 463 penalty minutes	940 goals 2,027 assists 2,967 points 596 penalty minutes

SIDNEY CROSBY

DEFENSEMAN

Duncan Keith, Blackhawks	Bobby Orr, Bruins/Blackhawks
6 feet 1 inch (185 cm) 196 pounds (89 kg)	6 feet (183 cm) 197 pounds (89 kg)
2005–present	1966–1979
65 goals 305 assists 370 points 445 penalty minutes	270 goals 645 assists 915 points 953 penalty minutes

GOALTENDER

Martin Brodeur, Devils	Terry Sawchuk, Red Wings/Bruins/Maple Leafs/Kings/Rangers
6 feet 2 inches (188 cm) 215 pounds (98 kg)	5 feet 11 inches (180 cm) 195 pounds (88 kg)
1991–present	1949–1970
688 wins 2.24 goals-against average	447 wins 2.51 goals-against average

TERRY SAWCHUK

*combined NHL/WHA stats

CHAPTER 5
TEAM RECORDS

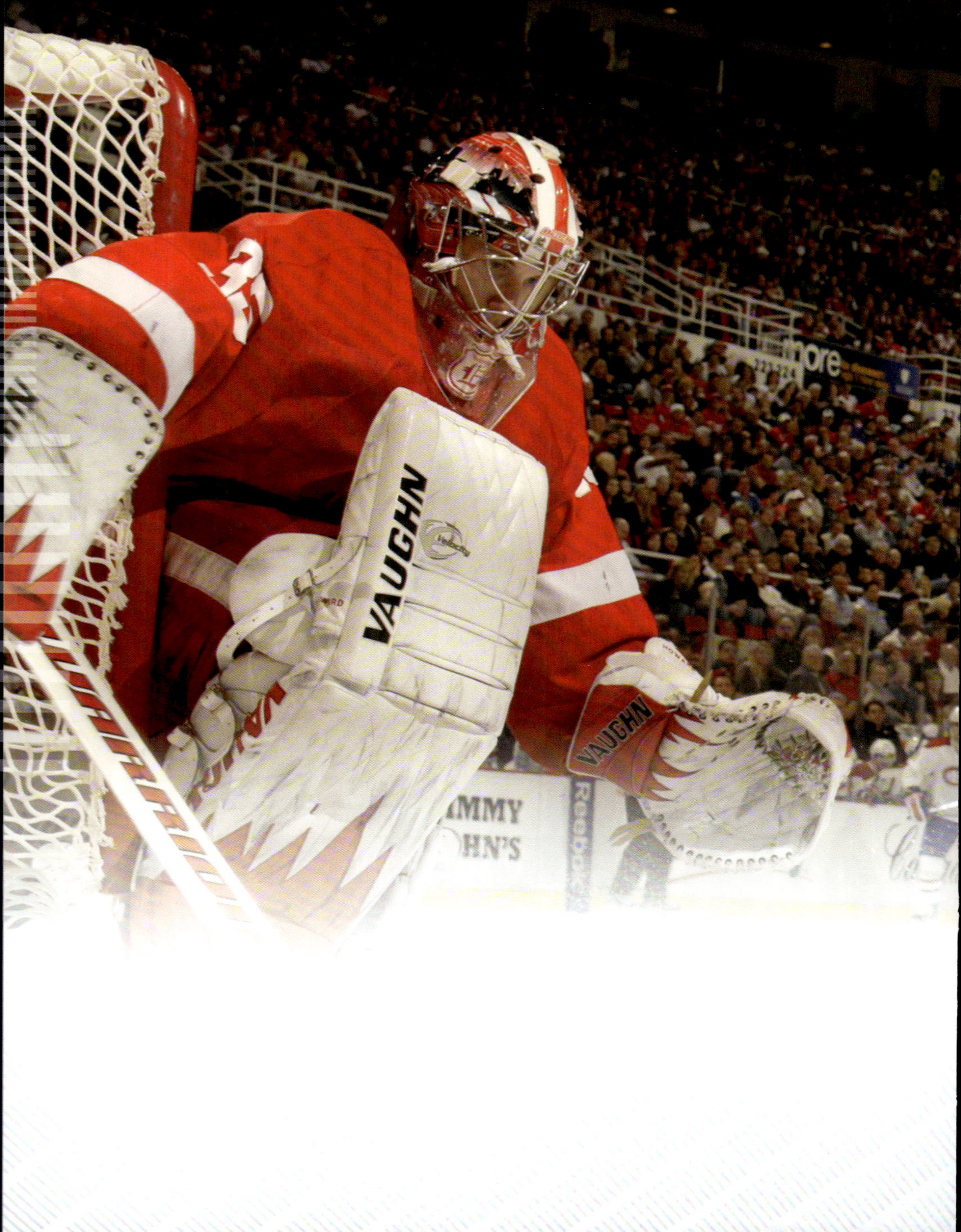

Hockey is considered to be one of the greatest team games. Goals are rarely scored without help—that's why assists are awarded. Goaltenders are aided by their defensemen and forwards' strong play at their own end of the rink. If it's all done well together, a team will be successful. The team's going to score goals. It's going to limit opponents' scoring chances. It's going to win games. And it has a chance to set records.

The best teams hold records for the most championships, the most wins, and the most points. Can you imagine what it would have been like to be an Edmonton Oilers fan in the 1980s? For five years in a row, they not only led the league in scoring, but they hit goal totals never seen before or since in NHL history. During the 1983–84 season, Edmonton scored 446 goals. In comparison, in 2011–12, the Pittsburgh Pengiuns led the league with 273 goals—173 fewer than the highest-scoring team of all time.

▼ Evgeni Malkin

MOST WINS (SINGLE SEASON)

1.	Detroit Red Wings	62	1995–96
2.	Montreal Canadiens	60	1976–77
3.	Montreal Canadiens	59	1977–78
4.	Detroit Red Wings	58	2005–06
	Montreal Canadiens	58	1975–76
6.	Boston Bruins	57	1970–71
	Edmonton Oilers	57	1983–84
8.	Edmonton Oilers	56	1985–86
	Pittsburgh Penguins	56	1992–93
10.	Eight teams tied with	54	

▲ Sergei Fedorov of the Detroit Red Wings

FEWEST WINS (SINGLE SEASON)

1.	Washington Capitals	8	1974–75
2.	Winnipeg Jets	9	1980–81
3.	Ottawa Senators	10	1992–93
4.	San Jose Sharks	11	1992–93
	Washington Capitals	11	1975–76
6.	Chicago Blackhawks	12	1953–54
	Kansas City Scouts	12	1975–76
	New York Islanders	12	1972–73
	Quebec Nordiques	12	1989–90
10.	Three teams tied with	13	

▲ Robert Picard of the Washington Capitals

RECORD FACT The most- and fewest-wins records come from the era in which the NHL played 70 games or more. The NHL schedule expanded from 60 to 70 games starting with the 1949–50 season.

STREAKS

▼ Philadelphia Flyers

Winning Streak: The Pittsburgh Penguins won 17 games in a row during the 1992–93 season.

Unbeaten Streak: The Philadelphia Flyers did not lose a game in 35 straight contests during the 1979–80 season, going 25–0–10.

Losing Streak: The longest losing streak is 17 games in a row, set by the Washington Capitals in 1974–75 and the San Jose Sharks in 1992–93.

Winless Streak: The Winnipeg Jets went 0–23–7, a streak of 30 games in a row without a win in the 1980–81 season.

MOST GOALS SCORED IN A SEASON

1.	Edmonton Oilers	446	1983–84
2.	Edmonton Oilers	426	1985–86
3.	Edmonton Oilers	424	1982–83
4.	Edmonton Oilers	417	1981–82
5.	Edmonton Oilers	401	1984–85
6.	Boston Bruins	399	1970–71
7.	Calgary Flames	397	1987–88
8.	Montreal Canadiens	387	1976–77
9.	New York Islanders	385	1981–82
10.	Los Angeles Kings	376	1988–89

▲ Wayne Gretzky of the Edmonton Oilers

RECORD FACT Only one team in NHL history has averaged less than one goal per game on offense. The 1928–29 Chicago Blackhawks scored just 33 goals in a 44-game season, an average of 0.75 goals per game.

MOST GOALS ALLOWED IN A SEASON

#	Team	Goals	Season
1.	Washington Capitals	446	1974–75
2.	Detroit Red Wings	415	1985–86
3.	San Jose Sharks	414	1992–93
4.	Quebec Nordiques	407	1989–90
5.	Hartford Whalers	403	1982–83
6.	Vancouver Canucks	401	1984–85
7.	Winnipeg Jets	400	1980–81
8.	Ottawa Senators	397	1993–94
9.	Ottawa Senators	395	1992–93
10.	Washington Capitals	394	1975–76
	Pittsburgh Penguins	394	1982–83

RECORD FACT The Montreal Canadiens defeated the Quebec Bulldogs 16-3 on March 3, 1920. No team since has scored 16 goals in a single game.

MOST GOALS IN A GAME (BOTH TEAMS)

#	Matchup	Total	Date
1.	Canadiens 14, St. Patricks 7	21	Jan. 10, 1920
	Oilers 12, Blackhawks 9	21	Dec. 11, 1985
3.	Oilers 12, North Stars 8	20	Jan. 4, 1984
	Maple Leafs 11, Oilers 9	20	Jan. 8, 1986
5.	Wanderers 10, Arenas 9	19	Dec. 19, 1917
	Canadiens 16, Bulldogs 3	19	March 3, 1920
	Canadiens 13, Tigers 6	19	Feb. 26, 1921
	Bruins 10, Rangers 9	19	March 4, 1944
	Red Wings 10, Bruins 9	19	March 16, 1944
	Canucks 10, North Stars 9	19	Oct. 7, 1983

SINGLE-PERIOD SCORING

The Buffalo Sabres set the record for most goals by a team in one period on March 19, 1981. In a 14-4 victory over the Toronto Maple Leafs, Buffalo scored nine goals in the second period. Toronto also scored three times that period. The 12 combined goals are tied for a record with the Edmonton Oilers and Chicago Blackhawks. The two teams each had six goals in a period during a 1985 game.

▼ Danny Gare of the Buffalo Sabres

CHAPTER 6: THE TEAMS

For many years there were only six teams in the NHL: the Boston Bruins, Chicago Blackhawks, Detroit Red Wings, Montreal Canadiens, New York Rangers, and Toronto Maple Leafs. In 1967 the league doubled in size. Over the next 33 years, 18 more teams joined the league, putting pro hockey in almost every major city in North America.

EASTERN CONFERENCE

Metropolitan Division

Carolina Hurricanes—In 1997 the Hurricanes moved from Hartford, Connecticut—where they were the Whalers—to Raleigh, North Carolina.

Columbus Blue Jackets—The Blue Jackets became Ohio's second NHL team when they joined the league in 2000; the Cleveland Barons lasted just two seasons before the franchise moved in the 1970s.

New Jersey Devils—The Devils started out in Kansas City as the Scouts before moving to Colorado as the Rockies and finally to New Jersey.

New York Islanders—The Islanders' Mike Bossy had nine 50-goal seasons for New York; he is the only player in history to have that many with the same team.

New York Rangers—The Rangers were not the first NHL team to play in New York City, but they survived after the New York/Brooklyn Americans folded.

Philadelphia Flyers—The NHL doubled in size, going from six teams to 12 in 1967. In 1974 the Flyers became the first of those new teams to win the Stanley Cup.

Pittsburgh Penguins—When Mario Lemieux came out of retirement in 2000, he became the first team owner to skate in an NHL game.

Washington Capitals—The Capitals' first season, 1974–1975, was the worst for any team in NHL history; they had a .131 winning percentage and lost 17 games in a row during one stretch.

Atlantic Division

Boston Bruins—The Bruins were the first U.S. team to join the NHL, which only had Canadian teams at the time.

Buffalo Sabres—The NHL decided to expand into Buffalo, New York, in 1970; the decision was based on the success of a minor-league team that played in that city for 30 years and won five championships.

Detroit Red Wings—Detroit's NHL team was called the Cougars for four years and then the Falcons for two years before settling on the Red Wings in 1932.

Florida Panthers—The Panthers won 33 games during their first season (1993–1994) in Florida, a record for an expansion team.

Montreal Canadiens—Only Major League Baseball's New York Yankees have won more professional championships (27) than the Canadiens, who have 24 Stanley Cups.

Ottawa Senators—The original Ottawa Senators existed from the late 1800s to 1935. In 1992 the NHL added a new team with the old name in Canada's capital city.

Tampa Bay Lightning—When they won the 2004 Cup, the Lightning became the southern-most team in the NHL to win a championship.

Toronto Maple Leafs—The Leafs were first called the Arenas and the St. Patricks before they got their current nickname in 1926.

WESTERN CONFERENCE

Central Division

Chicago Blackhawks—In 1937–1938 the Blackhawks went 14–25–9, yet won the Stanley Cup; it remains the worst record of any championship team.

Colorado Avalanche—The Avalanche won the Stanley Cup in 1995–1996, their first year in Denver after moving from Quebec City, where they were the Nordiques.

Dallas Stars—Mike Modano spent 20 seasons with the Stars—four when the team was in Minnesota—and became the NHL's top-scoring U.S.-born player.

Minnesota Wild—Before the first home game in franchise history, the Wild retired the number 1 in honor of their fans, who were without an NHL team for seven years.

Nashville Predators—The Predators got their nickname because the bones of a saber-toothed tiger were found in an underground cave near Nashville, Tennessee.

St. Louis Blues—The Blues played in the Stanley Cup finals in each of their first three seasons, losing to the Canadiens in 1968 and 1969 and the Bruins in 1970.

Winnipeg Jets—The Winnipeg Jets name resurfaced in 2012 when the Atlanta Thrashers moved to Winnipeg, Manitoba, Canada. The original Jets moved to Phoenix.

Pacific Division

Anaheim Ducks—The team was originally called the Mighty Ducks, named after a 1992 Disney movie about a youth hockey team.

Arizona Coyotes—Phoenix is one of many teams with a connection to Wayne Gretzky; he coached the Coyotes for four seasons and was once a partial owner of the Arizona team.

Calgary Flames—Three brothers from the Sutter family have coached the Flames: Brent, Brian, and Darryl; another brother—Ron Sutter—played for Calgary, as did Darryl's son, Brett.

Edmonton Oilers—During the Wayne Gretzky-led dynasty of the 1980s, the Oilers scored at least 400 goals five seasons in a row.

Los Angeles Kings—In 2012 the eighth-seeded Kings beat the New Jersey Devils to win their first Stanley Cup.

San Jose Sharks—The Sharks aren't the first NHL team to play in California's San Francisco Bay area; the Oakland Seals were part of the 1967 expansion class but lasted just nine years.

Vancouver Canucks—The Canucks are still waiting for their first Stanley Cup, but the city of Vancouver isn't; in 1915 a team called the Vancouver Millionaires won the trophy.

TRIVIA

Name the six NHL teams whose nicknames are animals.

Answer: Bruins (a bear), Coyotes, Ducks, Panthers, Penguins, Sharks

CHAMPIONS

Since the late 1800s, hockey teams have competed for the Stanley Cup, which goes to the sport's champion every year. The NHL was created in 1917, and the famous trophy became the ultimate prize for teams in the world's best hockey league. No team captured more Cups than the Montreal Canadiens, who have won it an amazing 24 times, including once before the NHL even existed.

STANLEY CUP CHAMPIONS

TEAM	YEARS WON
Montreal Canadiens	1916, 1924, 1930, 1931, 1944, 1946, 1953, 1956, 1957, 1958, 1959, 1960, 1965, 1966, 1968, 1969, 1971, 1973, 1976, 1977, 1978, 1979, 1986, 1993
Toronto Maple Leafs	1918, 1922, 1932, 1942, 1945, 1947, 1948, 1949, 1951, 1962, 1963, 1964, 1967
Detroit Red Wings	1936, 1937, 1943, 1950, 1952, 1954, 1955, 1997, 1998, 2002, 2008
Boston Bruins	1929, 1939, 1941, 1970, 1972, 2011
Edmonton Oilers	1984, 1985, 1987, 1988, 1990
Chicago Blackhawks	1934, 1938, 1961, 2010, 2013
New York Rangers	1928, 1933, 1940, 1994
New York Islanders	1980, 1981, 1982, 1983
New Jersey Devils	1995, 2000, 2003
Pittsburgh Penguins	1991, 1992, 2009
Colorado Avalanche	1996, 2001
Philadelphia Flyers	1974, 1975
Anaheim Ducks	2007
Calgary Flames	1989
Carolina Hurricanes	2006
Dallas Stars	1999
Los Angeles Kings	2012, 2014
Tampa Bay Lightning	2004

OTHER STANLEY CUP WINNERS—NHL ERA

| Ottawa Senators | 1921, 1923, 1927 | Montreal Maroons | 1926, 1935 |

OTHER STANLEY CUP WINNERS—PRE-NHL

Ottawa Silver Screen	1903*, 1904, 1905, 1906*
Montreal AAA	1893, 1894, 1902*, 1903*
Montreal Victorias	1895, 1896*, 1897, 1898, 1899*
Montreal Wanderers	1906*, 1907*, 1908, 1910
Winnipeg Victorias	1896*, 1901, 1902*
Montreal Shamrocks	1899*, 1900
Ottawa Senators	1909, 1911
Quebec Bulldogs	1912, 1913
Kenora Thistles	1907*
Seattle Metropolitans	1917
Toronto Blueshirts	1914
Vancouver Millionaires	1915

*Years the Stanley Cup was shared by leagues

THE MONTREAL AMATEUR ATHLETIC ASSOCIATION (AAA)

DYNASTIES

Every so often a team becomes so good that it dominates for several years in a row. Those eras are known as dynasties. The NHL recognizes nine dynasties throughout its history. Five franchises have made up those dynasties.

BRYAN TROTTIER

NEW YORK ISLANDERS

From 1979 to 1983, the Islanders made NHL history. They became the first franchise from the United States to win four straight Stanley Cups. Their first championship took place eight years after the team was added to the NHL. Seven Hall of Famers, including coach Al Arbour, were part of the historic teams, which had a 16–3 finals record.

TORONTO MAPLE LEAFS

The Maple Leafs captured four Stanley Cups, including three in a row, between 1946 and 1951. Thirteen Hall of Famers, including president Conn Smythe, were part of the Toronto team during that stretch. The Maple Leafs made another great run in the 1960s. They won four more Cups between 1961 and 1967. Sixteen Hall of Famers helped make the second Leafs dynasty possible.

MONTREAL CANADIENS

KEN DRYDEN

The Canadiens have won more Stanley Cups than any other team. They also put together three dynasties: 1956–1960, 1964–1969, and 1975–1979. Montreal's first dynasty included five consecutive Cup wins. Twelve players from that era are now in the Hall of Fame. The second dynasty included four more titles and many of the same players. The final dynasty won four Stanley Cups in a row and featured 11 Hall of Famers.

OTTAWA SENATORS

The Ottawa dynasty rose to power as the original Senators. Between 1919 and 1927, the Senators became the NHL's first dynasty. They won four Stanley Cups behind 14 future Hall of Famers. One of those players, King Clancy, played every position on the ice—including goaltender—during a 1923 Cup finals game.

EDMONTON OILERS

Edmonton Oilers center Wayne Gretzky

Having the great Wayne Gretzky was a big reason why the Oilers were a dynasty from 1983 to 1990. But Edmonton had so much more. In fact, when Edmonton won its fifth championship during the run, Gretzky had already been traded to the Los Angeles Kings. During both the 1983–1984 and the 1985–1986 seasons, the Oilers had three players with 50 goals or more and four players with 100 points or more. Six Hall of Famers led Edmonton on its great run.

GREATEST SEASONS

Each season one team stands tall after a grueling regular season and a hard-fought playoffs. With the Stanley Cup hoisted high, the players skate around the rink as NHL champions. But there are only a few teams that have had truly historic seasons. From star players to masterful coaching, these teams set NHL records that still stand today. It's easy to see why these teams are considered the greatest of all time.

MOST POINTS: 1976-1977
MONTREAL CANADIENS

During their 1970s dynasty, the Montreal Canadiens compiled one of the best seasons in NHL history. In 1976–1977 they went 60–8–12. They ended with a record 132 points for the regular-season standings (two points for wins, one point for ties). Right wing Guy Lafleur scored 56 goals and had 136 points, and Steve Shutt scored 60 goals. The Canadiens scored 216 more goals than their opponents. Montreal cruised through the playoffs, losing just twice and sweeping the Boston Bruins in the finals for its 20th Stanley Cup.

HIGHEST-SCORING TEAM: 1983–1984 EDMONTON OILERS

The 1983–1984 Oilers team was a well-oiled scoring machine. The first year they won a Stanley Cup, they set a scoring record with 446 goals—an average of more than 5.5 goals per game. Wayne Gretzky led the way with 87 goals and 205 points. Glenn Anderson and Jari Kurri scored more than 50 goals each. Kurri, Mark Messier, and defenseman Paul Coffey each had more than 100 points.

MOST WINS: 1995–1996 DETROIT RED WINGS

In 1995–1996 the Detroit Red Wings were dominant during the regular season, winning a record 62 games. They were led by top-scorer Sergei Fedorov, who had 107 points, and longtime captain Steve Yzerman, who had 95 points. Coach Scotty Bowman, who also coached the 1976–1977 Canadiens, was behind the bench. Detroit won the President's Trophy as the team with the best regular-season record. However, their great season was spoiled when they failed to win the Stanley Cup.

BEST WIN PERCENTAGE: 1929–1930 BOSTON BRUINS

In the 1920s and 1930, NHL teams played only 44 games in a season compared to 82 today. In 1929–1930 the Boston Bruins had what still stands as the league's record-best winning percentage. Behind great defenseman Eddie Shore, the team went 38–5–1 for a .875 success rate. Although the Bruins won the Stanley Cup a year earlier, they were unable to repeat in 1929–1930.

COACHES

They are known as the bench bosses, the ringmasters, and the geniuses behind the game. Coaches have the task of putting the right line combinations together, selecting the best goalies, and motivating their teams to play to their full potential.

SCOTTY BOWMAN

Scotty Bowman deserves a spot at the top of the list of greatest hockey coaches. He coached for 30 seasons and won 1,244 games—462 more victories than Al Arbour, the second coach on the list. Bowman won nine Stanley Cup championships—five with the Canadiens, three with the Red Wings, and one with the Penguins. Bowman won his first Stanley Cup in 1973 and his last in 2002.

AL ARBOUR

It didn't take long for the New York Islanders to go from an expansion team to an NHL dynasty. Coach Al Arbour is a big reason why. The coach took over the team in 1973, one year after the Islanders were created. By the end of the 1979–1980 season, they were Stanley Cup champions. New York also won the next three Cups behind Arbour. In 23 seasons Arbour compiled 782 wins, good enough for second on the all-time wins list.

HERB BROOKS

One of the great coaching jobs of all time didn't take place in the NHL. Although Herb Brooks coached in the NHL for seven seasons and had only two losing seasons, his triumphant moment came during the 1980 Olympics. He led Team USA to the greatest upset in sports history. During the "Miracle on Ice" the Americans defeated the mighty Soviet Union team in Lake Placid, New York. A master motivator, Brooks also won three college titles at the University of Minnesota.

Top Coaches

- Jack Adams, Red Wings/Cougars/Falcons—coach of the year trophy is named after the three-time Cup winner
- Al Arbour, Blues/Islanders—led Isles dynasty that won four championships in a row
- Mike Babcock, Ducks/Red Wings—Only coach to win a Stanley Cup, an Olympic gold medal, and a world championship.
- Toe Blake, Canadiens—won eight Cups with Montreal, including five in a row
- Scotty Bowman, Blues/Canadiens/Sabres/Penguins/Red Wings—won nine Stanley Cups, more than any other coach
- Hap Day, Maple Leafs—led Toronto to five Cup victories
- Punch Imlach, Maple Leafs/Sabres—oversaw the Leafs' second dynasty, winning four titles
- Dick Irvin, Blackhawks/Maple Leafs/Canadiens—won four Stanley Cups
- Mike Keenan, Flyers/Blackhawks/Rangers/Blues/Canucks/Bruins/Panthers/Flames—ranks fifth in all-time wins
- Glen Sather, Oilers/Rangers—won four championships with Edmonton dynasty

MIKE KEENAN

CHAPTER 7
PLAYOFF RECORDS

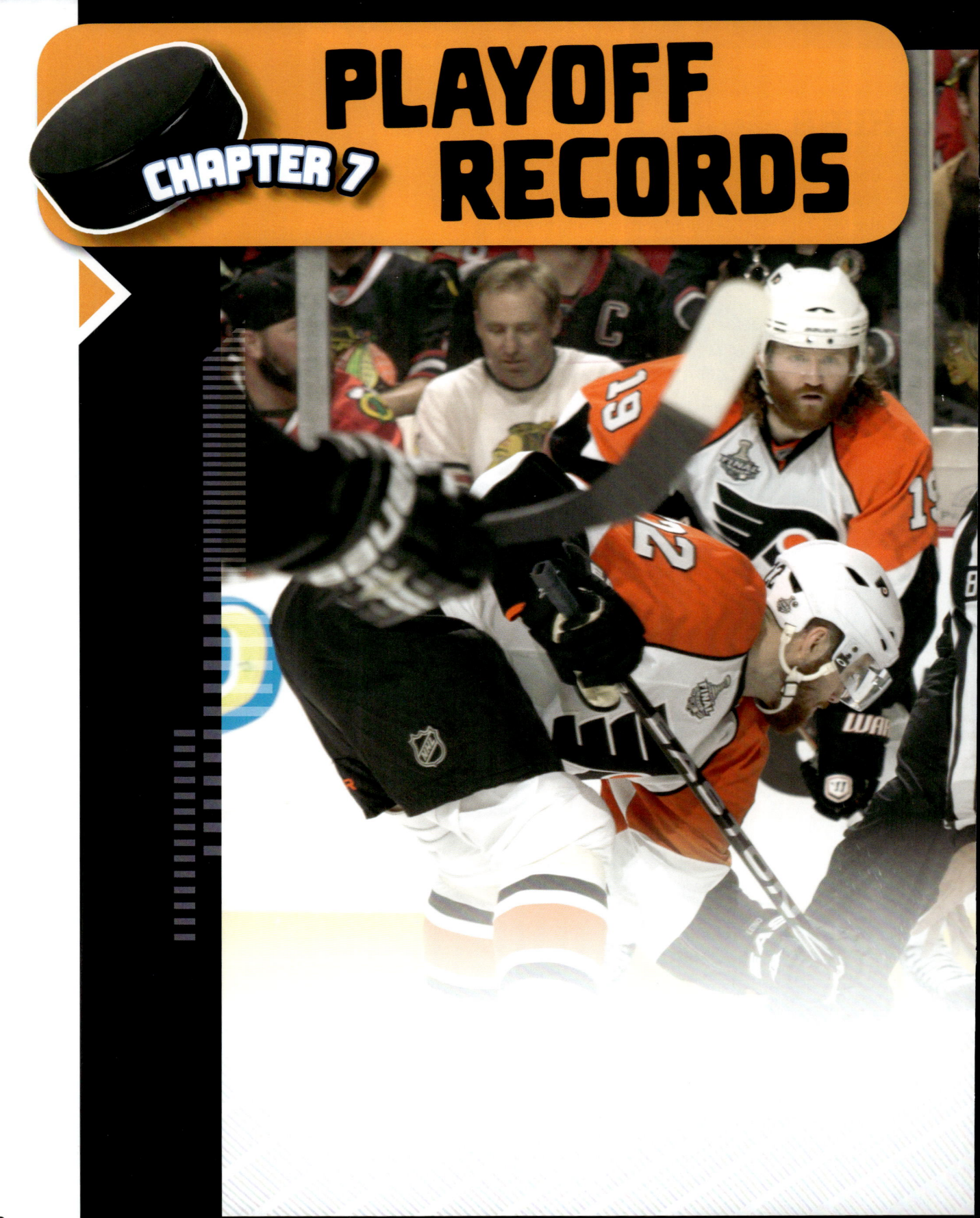

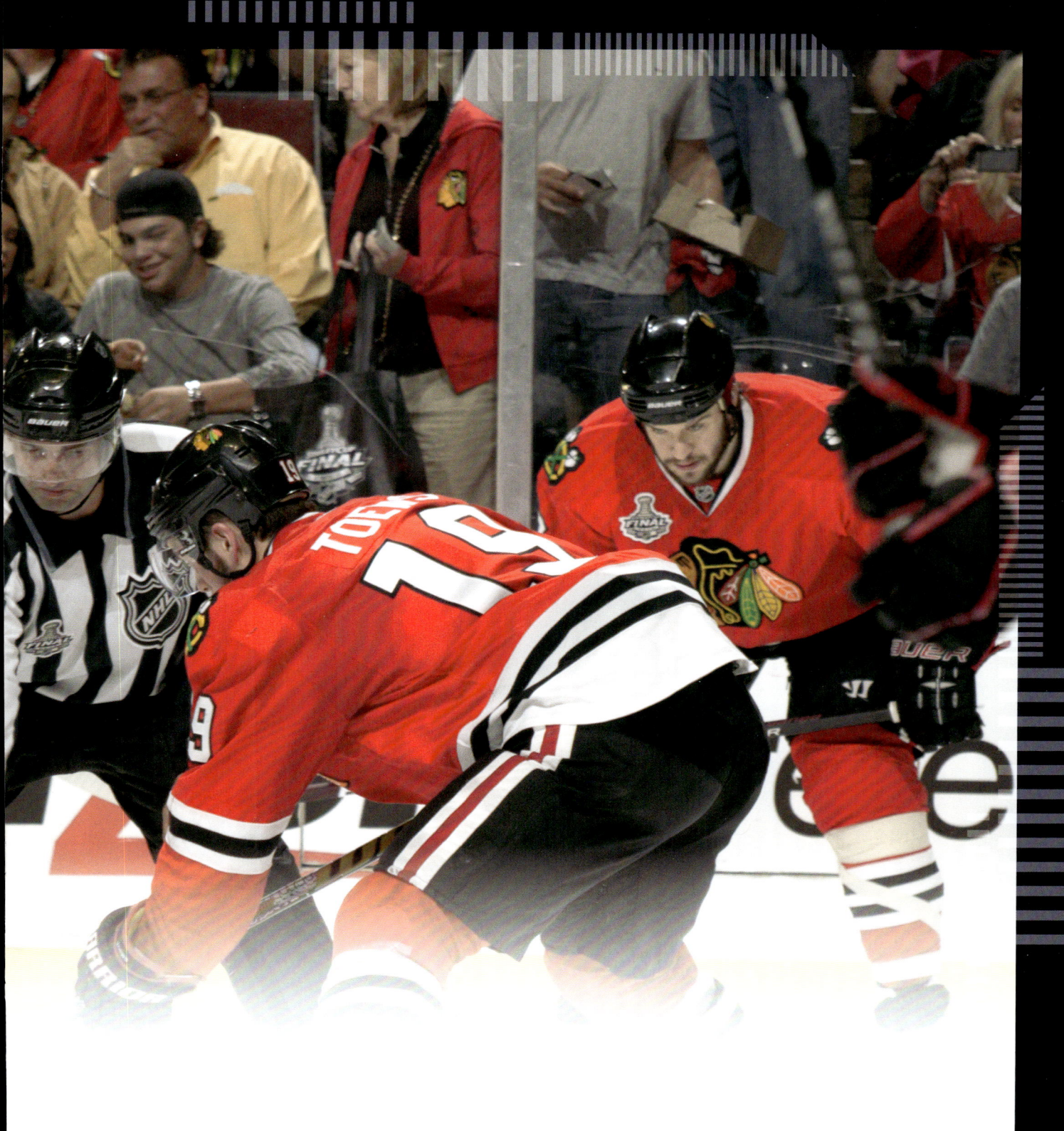

In the NHL every team starts the season aiming to make the playoffs. The ultimate prize is making it to the Stanley Cup finals and winning a championship. The postseason has featured many outstanding, memorable performances. Some of those performances have put players and teams into the record books. When a record leads to a championship, it's that much sweeter.

Tampa Bay Lightning forward Brad Richards won the Conn Smythe trophy in 2004 as the most valuable player of the playoffs—and for good reason. Not only did he lead the Lightning to its first Stanley Cup title, but he set an NHL record by scoring seven game-winning goals along the way.

If you ever wondered how good goaltender Patrick Roy was, look no further than his playoff records. No goalie in NHL history has played in more playoff games. His total of 247 appearances puts him third all-time among all players.

▼ Boston Bruins

MOST CHAMPIONSHIPS		
1.	Montreal Canadiens	23
2.	Toronto Maple Leafs	13
3.	Detroit Red Wings	11
4.	Boston Bruins	6
5.	Edmonton Oilers	5
	Chicago Blackhawks	5
7	New York Islanders	4
	New York Rangers	4
9.	New Jersey Devils	3
	Pittsburgh Penguins	3

▼ Montreal Canadiens

REPEAT CHAMPIONS

The Montreal Canadiens are the only team to win five consecutive championships, winning the Stanley Cup each year from 1956 through 1960. The Canadiens also won four in a row from 1976 through 1979. The only other team to win four in a row was the New York Islanders, champions from 1980 through 1983.

▲ New York Islanders

RECORD FACT The New York Islanders hold the record for consecutive playoff series wins. Between 1980 and 1984, they won 19 series in a row, including four Stanley Cups. They finally lost to the Edmonton Oilers in the 1984 Cup finals.

PLAYOFF APPEARANCES

1.	Montreal Canadiens	81
2.	Boston Bruins	69
3.	Toronto Maple Leafs	65
4.	Detroit Red Wings	62
5.	Chicago Blackhawks	59
6.	New York Rangers	56
7.	St. Louis Blues	38
8.	Philadelphia Flyers	37
9.	Dallas Stars	30
10.	Buffalo Sabres	29

▼ Boston Bruins

MOST CHAMPIONSHIPS WON (PLAYER)

1.	Henri Richard	11	Canadiens
2	Jean Beliveau	10	Canadiens
3.	Claude Provost	9	Canadiens
4.	Yvan Cournoyer	8	Canadiens
	Red Kelly	8	Red Wings/Maple Leafs
	Jacques Lemaire	8	Canadiens
	Maurice Richard	8	Canadiens
8.	Serge Savard	7	Canadiens
	Jean-Guy Talbot	7	Canadiens
10.	Many others tied with	6	

▲ Henri Richard

RECORD FACT No player has appeared in more games without winning the Stanley Cup than Phil Housley. He played in 1,495 games over 21 seasons. The closest he came to a championship was in 1998, but his Washington Capitals lost to the Detroit Red Wings in the Cup finals.

PLAYOFF GOALS

▼ Jari Kurri

CAREER

1.	Wayne Gretzky	122	Oilers/Kings/Blues/Rangers	16 playoffs
2.	Mark Messier	109	Oilers/Rangers/Canucks	17 playoffs
3.	Jari Kurri	106	Oilers/Kings/Rangers/Ducks/Avalanche	15 playoffs
4.	Brett Hull	103	Flames/Blues/Stars/Red Wings/Coyotes	19 playoffs
5.	Glenn Anderson	93	Oilers/Maple Leafs/Rangers/Blues	15 playoffs
6.	Mike Bossy	85	Islanders	10 playoffs
7.	Joe Sakic	84	Nordiques/Avalanche	13 playoffs
8.	Maurice Richard	82	Canadiens	15 playoffs
9.	Claude Lemieux	80	Canadiens/Devils/Avalanche/Coyotes/Stars/Sharks	18 playoffs
10.	Jean Beliveau	79	Canadiens	17 playoffs

SINGLE SEASON

1.	Jari Kurri	19	Oilers	1985
	Reggie Leach	19	Flyers	1976
3.	Joe Sakic	18	Avalanche	1996
4.	Mike Bossy	17	Islanders	1981
	Mike Bossy	17	Islanders	1982
	Mike Bossy	17	Islanders	1983
	Wayne Gretzky	17	Oilers	1985
	Steve Payne	17	North Stars	1981
	Kevin Stevens	17	Penguins	1991
10.	Six players tied with	16		

▲ Joe Sakic

CLUTCH SCORERS

Five players have scored five goals in a single playoff game.

Newsy Lalonde	Montreal Canadiens	1919
Maurice Richard	Montreal Canadiens	1944
Darryl Sittler	Toronto Maple Leafs	1976
Reggie Leach	Philadelphia Flyers	1976
Mario Lemieux	Pittsburgh Penguins	1989

▲ Maurice Richard

PLAYOFF POWER-PLAY GOALS (SINGLE SEASON)

1.	Mike Bossy	9	Islanders	1981
	Cam Neely	9	Bruins	1991
3.	John Druce	8	Capitals	1990
	Tim Kerr	8	Flyers	1989
	Mario Lemieux	8	Penguins	1992
	Brian Propp	8	North Stars	1991
7.	Several players tied with	7		

▲ Mario Lemieux

RECORD FACT Six players have scored three short-handed goals during a playoff run. Naturally, Wayne Gretzky was one of them, accomplishing the feat in 1983. Bill Barber, Lorne Henning, Todd Marchant, Wayne Presley, and Derek Sanderson complete the list.

PLAYOFF GAME-WINNING GOALS (SINGLE SEASON)

1.	Brad Richards	7	Lightning	2004
2.	Joe Nieuwendyk	6	Stars	1999
	Joe Sakic	6	Avalanche	1996
4.	Mike Bossy	5	Islanders	1983
	Dustin Byfuglien	5	Blackhawks	2010
	Johan Franzen	5	Red Wings	2008
	Jari Kurri	5	Oilers	1987
	Mario Lemieux	5	Penguins	1992
	Fernando Pisani	5	Oilers	2006
	Bobby Smith	5	North Stars	1991

▼ Dustin Byfuglien

RECORD FACT Wayne Gretzky and Brett Hull have scored more game-winning playoff goals than any other players. Each netted 24 winners in his career. Joe Sakic has the record for overtime game-winners, scoring eight in his playoff career.

OVERTIME WINNERS

Sixteen players in NHL history have scored a goal in overtime that gave their team the Stanley Cup championship. In 2014, the Los Angeles Kings' Alec Martinez scored with 5:17 remaining in the second overtime to clinch the cup against the New York Rangers. Two players, Brett Hull of the Dallas Stars in 1999 and Uwe Krupp of the Colorado Avalanche in 1996, won the Cup with a goal in triple overtime. Only two finals have gone beyond the distance, going into overtime in Game 7. The Detroit Red Wings won both of those games, with Pete Babando scoring in double overtime in 1950 and Tony Leswick scoring in overtime for the 1954 championship.

▲ Patrick Kane

PLAYOFF ASSISTS

CAREER

1.	Wayne Gretzky	260	Oilers/Kings/Blues/Rangers	16 playoffs
2.	Mark Messier	186	Oilers/Rangers/Canucks	17 playoffs
3.	Ray Bourque	139	Bruins/Avalanche	21 playoffs
4.	Paul Coffey	137	Oilers/Penguins/Kings/Red Wings/Whalers/Flyers/Blackhawks/Hurricanes/Bruins	16 playoffs
5.	Nicklas Lidstrom	129	Red Wings	20 playoffs
6.	Doug Gilmour	128	Blues/Flames/Maple Leafs/Devils/Blackhawks/Sabres/Canadiens	17 playoffs
7.	Jari Kurri	127	Oilers/Kings/Rangers/Ducks/Avalanche	15 playoffs
8.	Sergei Fedorov	124	Red Wings/Ducks/Blue Jackets/Capitals	15 playoffs
9.	Glenn Anderson	121	Oilers/Maple Leafs/Rangers/Blues	15 playoffs
	Al MacInnis	121	Flames/Blues	19 playoffs
	Jaromir Jagr	121	Penguins/Capitals/Rangers/Flyers/Bruins	17 playoffs

SINGLE SEASON

1.	Wayne Gretzky	31	Oilers	1988
2.	Wayne Gretzky	30	Oilers	1985
3.	Wayne Gretzky	29	Oilers	1987
4.	Mario Lemieux	28	Penguins	1991
5.	Wayne Gretzky	26	Oilers	1983
6.	Paul Coffey	25	Oilers	1985
	Doug Gilmour	25	Maple Leafs	1993
	Wayne Gretzky	25	Kings	1993
9.	Al MacInnis	24	Flames	1989
	Mark Recchi	24	Penguins	1991

▲ Wayne Gretzky

RECORD FACT Wayne Gretzky of the Edmonton Oilers and Mikko Leinonen of the New York Rangers each had a six-assist playoff game. Leinonen accomplished the feat in 1982, and Gretzky did it in 1987.

PLAYOFF POINTS

CAREER

1.	Wayne Gretzky	382	Oilers/Kings/Blues/Rangers	16 playoffs
2.	Mark Messier	295	Oilers/Rangers/Canucks	17 playoffs
3.	Jari Kurri	233	Oilers/Kings/Rangers/Ducks/Avalanche	15 playoffs
4.	Glenn Anderson	214	Oilers/Maple Leafs/Rangers/Blues	15 playoffs
5.	Jaromir Jagr	199	Penguins/Caps/Rangers/Flyers/Bruins	17 playoffs*
6.	Paul Coffey	196	Oilers/Penguins/Kings/Red Wings/Whalers/Flyers/Blackhawks/Hurricanes/Bruins	16 playoffs
7.	Brett Hull	190	Flames/Blues/Stars/Red Wings/Coyotes	19 playoffs
8.	Doug Gilmour	188	Blues/Flames/Maple Leafs/Devils/Blackhawks/Sabres/Canadiens	17 playoffs
	Joe Sakic	188	Nordiques/Avalanche	13 playoffs
10.	Steve Yzerman	185	Red Wings	20 playoffs

*Active player

SINGLE SEASON

1.	Wayne Gretzky	47	Oilers	1985
2.	Mario Lemieux	44	Penguins	1991
3.	Wayne Gretzky	43	Oilers	1988
4.	Wayne Gretzky	40	Kings	1993
5.	Wayne Gretzky	38	Oilers	1983
6.	Paul Coffey	37	Oilers	1985
7.	Evgeni Malkin	36	Penguins	2009
8.	Mike Bossy	35	Islanders	1981
	Doug Gilmour	35	Maple Leafs	1993
	Wayne Gretzky	35	Oilers	1984

▲ Paul Coffey

RECORD FACT The record for points in a single playoff game is eight, set by two players. Patrik Sundstrom of the New Jersey Devils earned eight points during a 1988 playoff game. Mario Lemieux of the Penguins matched the feat in 1989.

PLAYOFF GAMES (CAREER)

#	Player	Games	Teams	Playoffs
1.	Chris Chelios	266	Canadiens/Blackhawks/Red Wings	24 playoffs
2.	Nicklas Lidstrom	263	Red Wings	20 playoffs
3.	Patrick Roy	247	Canadiens/Avalanche	17 playoffs
4.	Mark Messier	236	Oilers/Rangers/Canucks	17 playoffs
5.	Claude Lemieux	234	Canadiens/Devils/Avalanche/Coyotes/Stars/Sharks	18 playoffs
6.	Scott Stevens	233	Capitals/Blues/Devils	20 playoffs
7.	Guy Carbonneau	231	Canadiens/Blues/Stars	17 playoffs
8.	Larry Robinson	227	Canadiens/Kings	20 playoffs
9.	Glenn Anderson	225	Oilers/Maple Leafs/Rangers/Blues	15 playoffs
10.	Kris Draper	222	Jets/Red Wings	18 playoffs

PLAYOFF GAMES BY A GOALIE (CAREER)

#	Player	Games	Teams	Playoffs
1.	Patrick Roy	247	Canadiens/Avalanche	17 playoffs
2.	Martin Brodeur	205	Devils	17 playoffs*
3.	Ed Belfour	161	Blackhawks/Stars/Maple Leafs	13 playoffs
4.	Grant Fuhr	150	Oilers/Sabres/Blues	14 playoffs
5.	Mike Vernon	138	Flames/Red Wings/Sharks/Panthers	14 playoffs
6.	Curtis Joseph	133	Blues/Oilers/Maple Leafs/Red Wings/Flames	14 playoffs
7.	Andy Moog	132	Oilers/Bruins/Stars/Canadiens	16 playoffs
	Billy Smith	132	Kings/Islanders	13 playoffs
9.	Chris Osgood	129	Red Wings/Islanders/Blues	13 playoffs
10.	Tom Barrasso	119	Sabres/Penguins/Senators	13 playoffs
	Dominik Hasek	119	Blackhawks/Sabres/Red Wings	13 playoffs

▲ Nicklas Lidstrom

*Active player

GOALIE PLAYOFF WINS (CAREER)

#	Player	Wins	Teams	Playoffs
1.	Patrick Roy	151	Canadiens/Avalanche	17 playoffs
2.	Martin Brodeur	113	Devils	17 playoffs*
3.	Grant Fuhr	92	Oilers/Sabres/Blues	14 playoffs
4.	Ed Belfour	88	Blackhawks/Stars/Maple Leafs	13 playoffs
	Billy Smith	88	Kings/Islanders	13 playoffs
6.	Ken Dryden	80	Canadiens	8 playoffs
7.	Mike Vernon	77	Flames/Red Wings/Sharks/Panthers	14 playoffs
8.	Chris Osgood	74	Red Wings/Islanders/Blues	13 playoffs
9.	Jacques Plante	71	Canadiens	16 playoffs
10.	Andy Moog	68	Oilers/Bruins/Stars/Canadiens	16 playoffs

*Active player

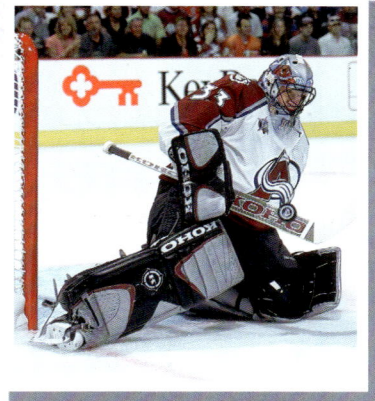

▼ Patrick Roy

THE STANLEY CUP

The oldest and most famous trophy in professional sports in North America is the Stanley Cup. It goes to the NHL champion each year. One of the things that makes the Cup special is that each member of the winning team gets his name engraved on it. The name of Henri Richard of the Montreal Canadiens is etched into the silver trophy 11 times—more than any other player. But Jean Beliveau of the Canadiens has his name on it more than any other person. It's on there 10 times as a player and another seven as a member of the team's management. Another layer is added to the cup when there's no more space to add names.

▼ Zdeno Chara with the Stanley Cup

PLAYOFF GOALS-AGAINST AVERAGE

▼ Patrick Lalime

CAREER

1.	Lorne Chabot	1.54	Rangers/Maple Leafs/Canadiens/Blackhawks/Maroons	9 playoffs
2.	Dave Kerr	1.74	Maroons/Rangers	9 playoffs
3.	Patrick Lalime	1.77	Senators	4 playoffs
4.	Clint Benedict	1.86	Senators/Maroons	8 playoffs
5.	Tiny Thompson	1.88	Bruins/Red Wings	10 playoffs
6.	Gerry McNeil	1.89	Canadiens	5 playoffs
	John Ross Roach	1.89	St. Patricks/Rangers/Red Wings	7 playoffs
8.	George Hainsworth	1.93	Canadiens/Maple Leafs	10 playoffs
9.	Turk Broda	1.98	Maple Leafs	13 playoffs
10.	Dominik Hasek	2.02	Blackhawks/Sabres/Red Wings	13 playoffs

SINGLE SEASON

1.	Alec Connell	0.60	Senators	1927
	Tiny Thompson	0.60	Bruins	1929
3.	Terry Sawchuk	0.63	Red Wings	1952
4.	George Hainsworth	0.75	Canadiens	1930
5.	John Ross Roach	0.77	Rangers	1929
6.	Clint Benedict	0.87	Maroons	1928
7.	Dave Kerr	1.09	Rangers	1937
8.	Turk Broda	1.10	Maple Leafs	1951
9.	Alec Connell	1.12	Maroons	1935
10.	Tiny Thompson	1.23	Bruins	1933

▲ Terry Sawchuk

PLAYOFF SAVE PERCENTAGE

CAREER

1.	Tim Thomas	.933	Bruins/Stars	5 playoffs*
2.	Jonas Hiller	.932	Ducks	4 playoffs*
3.	Tukka Rask	.930	Bruins	3 playoffs*
4.	Olaf Kolzig	.927	Capitals	6 playoffs
5.	Patrick Lalime	.926	Senators	4 playoffs*
6.	Jean-Sebastien Giguere	.925	Ducks	5 playoffs*
	Dominik Hasek	.925	Blackhawks/Sabres/Red Wings	13 playoffs
8.	Jonathan Quick	.923	Kings	5 playoffs*
9.	Henrik Lundqvist	.922	Rangers	8 playoffs*
10.	Miikka Kiprusoff	.921	Sharks/Flames	7 playoffs*

*Active player

▲ Jean-Sebastien Giguere

SINGLE SEASON

1.	Marty Turco	.952	Stars	2007
2.	Dominik Hasek	.950	Sabres	1994
3.	Jean-Sebastien Giguere	.946	Ducks	2003
	Kelly Hrudey	.946	Islanders	1985
	Patrick Lalime	.946	Senators	2002
	Jonathan Quick	.946	Kings	2012
7.	Ron Tugnutt	.945	Penguins	2000
8.	Ilya Bryzgalov	.944	Ducks	2006
	Mike Smith	.944	Coyotes	2012
10.	Jonas Hiller	.943	Ducks	2009
	Glen Hanlon	.943	Red Wings	1987

▲ Marty Turco

PLAYOFF SHUTOUTS

CAREER

1.	Martin Brodeur	24	Devils	17 playoffs*
2.	Patrick Roy	23	Canadiens/Avalanche	17 playoffs
3.	Curtis Joseph	16	Blues/Oilers/Maple Leafs/Red Wings/Flames	14 playoffs
4.	Chris Osgood	15	Red Wings/Islanders/Blues	13 playoffs
5.	Jacques Plante	14	Canadiens/Blues/Maple Leafs/Bruins	16 playoffs
	Dominik Hasek	14	Blackhawks/Sabres/Red Wings	13 playoffs
	Ed Belfour	14	Blackhawks/Stars/Maple Leafs	13 playoffs
8.	Turk Broda	13	Maple Leafs	13 playoffs
9.	Terry Sawchuk	12	Red Wings/Maple Leafs/Kings/Rangers	15 playoffs
10.	Ken Dryden	10	Canadiens	8 playoffs

*Active player

▼ Dominik Hasek

HIGHEST-SCORING GAMES

The Los Angeles Kings defeated the Edmonton Oilers 10-8 on April 7, 1982. The 18 goals were the most scored by two teams in a playoff game. In 1989 the Pittsburgh Penguins defeated the Philadelphia Flyers 10-7. The most goals scored by one team in a playoff game is 13, racked up by the Oilers in a 13-3 win over the Kings April 9, 1987.

▼ Marcel Dionne of the Los Angeles Kings

PLAYOFF SHUTOUTS

SINGLE SEASON

1.	Martin Brodeur	7	Devils	2003
2.	Dominik Hasek	6	Red Wings	2002
3.	Miikka Kiprusoff	5	Flames	2004
	Nikolai Khabibulin	5	Lightning	2004
	Jean-Sebastien Giguere	5	Ducks	2003
6.	Many players tied with	4		

▼ **Nikolai Khabibulin**

PLAYING TILL THE END

One of the most exciting things about playoff hockey is the fact that there are no ties or shootouts. Overtime games are played until a goal is scored. For the game's two goalies, all of the pressure is on them. In Stanley Cup playoff history, Ed Belfour has won more overtime games than any other goaltender. His 20 overtime wins include a triple-overtime victory in Game 6 of the 1999 finals that clinched the Stanley Cup. A year later, though, he gave up the Cup-winning goal to Jason Arnott of the New Jersey Devils.

▼ **Jason Arnott**

CHAPTER 8 FAN FAVORITES

ARENAS

OUT WITH THE OLD

The NHL's Original Six teams—the Canadiens, Maple Leafs, Bruins, Blackhawks, Red Wings, and Rangers—played in magnificent old buildings for most of their history. Those arenas included the Montreal Forum, Maple Leaf Gardens, Boston Garden, Chicago Stadium, the Detroit Olympia Stadium, and an older version of Madison Square Garden. The teams have since moved from those old "barns" and into state-of-the-art arenas. One of the oldest arenas in the NHL is Nassau Veterans Memorial Coliseum, home to the Islanders since 1972.

DETROIT RED WINGS' JOE LOUIS ARENA

MINNESOTA WILD'S XCEL ENERGY CENTER

IN WITH THE NEW

Many new arenas have been built for NHL teams in recent years. The newest building is the Penguins' Consol Energy Center, which the team moved into in 2010. Many surveys have named the Minnesota Wild's Xcel Energy Center as the best building in the league for both fans and players—of all ages. Besides being home to the self-proclaimed State of Hockey's professional team, it is also home to a college hockey championship and the boys and girls high school state championships.

SIT IN THE SADDLE

One of the most unique NHL arenas is the Flames' Scotiabank Saddledome. Why is it called the Saddledome? Because it looks like a giant could straddle the building and ride it across western Canada. Like a saddle atop a horse, the building has a low middle and high ends. The Saddledome was the site of Olympic hockey and figure skating in 1988, and the Flames played in three Stanley Cup Finals series there.

ON FROZEN POND

Each year the NHL honors hockey's outdoor beginnings by playing a New Year's Day game outside in the cold—and sometimes the snow. The NHL Winter Classic isn't played on lakes or rivers, though. A rink is set up in an outdoor stadium. The first was played in 2008 in Buffalo's Ralph Wilson Stadium. Then it went to a pair of historic baseball stadiums: Chicago's Wrigley Field in 2009 and Boston's Fenway Park in 2010.

WRIGLEY FIELD, 2009 NHL WINTER CLASSIC

Five Largest Hockey Arenas

1. Bell Centre (Canadiens)	21,273
2. Joe Louis Arena (Red Wings)	20,066
3. United Center (Blackhawks)	19,717
4. Wells Fargo Center (Flyers)	19,519
5. Tampa Bay Times Forum (Lightning)	19,500

NHL TROPHIES

The NHL is known for its trophies, which it hands out to its best players every season. The Hart Trophy has been given out to the league MVP since 1924, and the Conn Smythe Trophy has gone to the best player in the playoffs since 1965.

STANLEY CUP

No trophy in hockey—perhaps in any sport—is as famous as the Stanley Cup. The Cup is awarded to the team that wins the NHL playoff championship every season. The oldest trophy in professional sports, the Cup was first donated to hockey in 1892 by Sir Frederick Arthur Stanley, known as Lord Stanley of Preston. When a team wins the Cup, each player's name is engraved on the silver trophy, and each player gets to take it home for one day in the offseason.

STANLEY CUP FACTS

- The Canadiens' Henri Richard had his name engraved on the Cup a record 11 times as a player.

- Jean Beliveau has his name on the Cup 17 times as both a player and coach.

- Scotty Bowman won the Cup a record nine times as a coach.

- The first team to engrave its roster on the Cup was the Montreal Wanderers in 1907.

- The Cup is 35 ¼ inches (90 cm) high and weighs 34 ½ pounds (15.6 kg). It continues to grow because sections are added to fit the names of the new champions.

NHL AWARD TROPHIES

Art Ross Trophy
leading point scorer

Bill Masterton Memorial Trophy
player who displays perseverance and dedication to hockey

Calder Memorial Trophy
rookie of the year

Conn Smythe Trophy
most valuable player of the playoffs

Cam Ward with the 2006 Conn Smythe Trophy

Frank J. Selke Trophy
top defensive forward

Hart Memorial Trophy
most valuable player

Jack Adams Award
coach of the year

James Norris Memorial Trophy
top defenseman

King Clancy Memorial Trophy
player who displays leadership on the ice and in the community

Lady Byng Memorial Trophy
player who displays gentlemanly conduct

Maurice "Rocket" Richard Trophy
leading goal scorer

Ted Lindsay Award
MVP as voted on by the players

Vezina Trophy
top goaltender

William M. Jennings Trophy
goaltender with the lowest goals-against average

GREAT NICKNAMES

From "Mr. Hockey" Gordie Howe and "The Great One" Wayne Gretzky to Sid "The Kid" Crosby, hockey players are known for their nicknames. Rarely do players get called by their birth names when they're on the rink. Some nicknames have stuck throughout NHL history.

SID "THE KID" CROSBY

"THE GOLDEN JET" BOBBY HULL

In an era before helmets, Bobby Hull was known for his fast skating and his flowing blond hair.

BERNIE "BOOM BOOM" GEOFFRION

The Canadiens star of the 1950s got his great nickname from the sound that is made by the shot he supposedly invented—the slap shot.

MAURICE "ROCKET" RICHARD

The Canadiens' star was known for his intensity and speed, skating like a rocket around the Montreal Forum. He went to the All-Star Game 13 times and entered the NHL Hall of Fame in 1961.

"MR. ZERO" FRANK BRIMSEK

As a goalie with the Bruins in 1939–1940, Frank Brimsek earned his nickname by recording 10 shutouts and a pair of amazing scoreless streaks. One streak lasted 231 minutes, 54 seconds, and another spanned 220 minutes, 24 seconds en route to a Stanley Cup. He had 40 shutouts in his 10-year career.

DAVE "THE HAMMER" SCHULTZ

One of the great fighters in NHL history, Dave Schultz was one of the Flyers' famed "Broad Street Bullies." He led the NHL in penalty minutes four times during his career.

TRIVIA

Can you match these 10 nicknames to the correct player?

1. The Wrecking Ball		Al Arbour
2. The Red Baron		Gordon Berenson
3. The Monster		Derek Boogard
4. The Russian Rocket		Adam Brown
5. The Flying Scotsman		Pavel Bure
6. Radar		Johan Franzen
7. The Finnish Flash		Jonas Gustavsson
8. Cyclone		Mark Recchi
9. The Boogie Man		Teemu Selanne
10. The Mule		Marvin Wentworth

Answer: 1. Mark Recchi 2. Gordon Berenson 3. Jonas Gustavsson 4. Pavel Bure 5. Adam Brown 6. Al Arbour 7. Teemu Selanne 8. Marvin Wentworth 9. Derek Boogaard 10. Johan Franzen

OUTSIDE THE NHL

OLYMPIC HOCKEY

The NHL isn't the only place to showcase the great game of hockey. Some of the most exciting moments on the ice have taken place during the Winter Olympics.

The United States men's hockey team has won two gold medals, one in 1960 and one in 1980. In 1980 the young U.S. team pulled off the "Miracle on Ice." Behind the heroics of captain Mike Eruzione and goalie Jim Craig, the U.S. upset the favored Soviet Union 4-3. Eruzione scored the game-winning goal, and Craig made 39 saves. Two days later the Americans defeated Finland 4-2 for the gold medal.

In 2010 in Vancouver, British Columbia, Canada, the United States men played in one of the most memorable Olympic hockey games. In the early rounds of the Olympic tournament, the Americans upset the Canadians 5-3. In a final-game rematch Canada took an early lead and held it for most of the game. The game headed to overtime after U.S. forward Zach Parise tied the game with 25 seconds left in regulation. Penguins star Sidney Crosby gave the Canadians the gold medal with a thrilling goal in sudden-death overtime. Canada won Olympic gold again in 2014 in Sochi, Russia.

USA'S 1980 OLYMPIC HOCKEY TEAM

CANADA'S 2010 MEN'S OLYMPIC HOCKEY TEAM

WOMEN'S HOCKEY

Women and girls play at many levels: youth, high school, college, and international play. The NHL has expressed interest in creating a professional hockey league for women as well. Women's hockey has been an Olympic sport since 1998, when the United States won the gold medal in Nagano, Japan. Canada has won the last four gold medals, with the U.S. taking silver in 2002, 2010 and 2014. In Sochi, Russia, Canada made a stunning third-period comeback and won gold on Marie-Philip Poulin's goal in overtime.

Women's Canadian gold medal hockey team, 2010

COLLEGE HOCKEY

A popular level of hockey in the United States is the college game. The game is played mostly in the West, Midwest, and the Northeast. Some NHL stars who have won the Hobey Baker Award as college hockey's best player include Neal Broten (Minnesota, 1981), Paul Kariya (Maine, 1993), Chris Drury (Boston University, 1998), and Ryan Miller (Michigan State, 2001).

Boston College versus University of Wisconsin, 2010 NCAA Men's National Championship

RECENT NCAA DIVISION 1 WINNERS

Men's		Women's	
2014	Union Dutchmen	2014	Clarkson Golden Knights
2013	Yale Bulldogs	2013	Minnesota Golden Gophers
2012	Boston College Eagles	2012	Minnesota Golden Gophers
2011	Minnesota-Duluth Bulldogs	2011	Wisconsin Badgers
2010	Boston College Eagles	2010	Minnesota-Duluth Bulldogs
2009	Boston University Terriers	2009	Wisconsin Badgers

AROUND THE NHL

MASKED MEN

CHRIS MASON

Goalies are some of the game's most interesting characters. One place where they show off their personality is on their protective masks. Many of the masks have detailed pictures painted on the helmets. The Buffalo Sabres' Ryan Miller's helmet features the head of a red-eyed, blue-and-yellow buffalo. Former New York Rangers goalie Mike Richter had the head of the Statue of Liberty on his mask. Two fearsome skeletons creep along the helmet of Evgeni Nabokov of the San Jose Sharks.

EVGENI NABOKOV

BREAKING BARRIERS

On January 18, 1958, history was made when Bruins winger Willie O'Ree took the ice. O'Ree was the first black player to participate in an NHL game. The Canada native had a short professional career. He played in just two games that season and 43 games in 1960–1961 when he scored four goals. In 1992 the Lightning made history when they signed goaltender Manon Rheaume to a contract. She was the first and only woman to play in the NHL. Her only NHL playing time came during an exhibition game, but she also had a short minor-league career.

A REAL DREAM TEAM

In 1987 Canada put together one of the finest hockey teams ever assembled to compete for the Canada Cup. Long before NHL players were allowed to skate in the Olympics, the Canada Cup was an international tournament featuring pro players. Imagine a team with Mario Lemieux passing to Wayne Gretzky and back to Lemieux for a goal. Canada also had Mark Messier at forward, Paul Coffey on defense, and Grant Fuhr in front of the net. "For me," Gretzky said, "it was probably the best hockey I've ever played."

ROLLER HOCKEY

You don't need ice to play hockey. It can be played on wheels too. Some people play roller hockey outdoors in the summer. Others play indoors on specially made roller-skating surfaces. There is even a professional inline-skate league called Major League Roller Hockey. The league has teams in Chicago, Philadelphia, Washington, and other cities. Nashville Predators forward Joel Ward played roller hockey before working his way to the NHL.

MASCOTS

Hockey mascots add even more entertainment to an already exciting sport. They liven up the crowd with loud, energetic cheers. They provide comic relief by humorously falling over or pulling pranks on the refs or members of the other team. Some mascots, such as Al the Octopus, were created by traditions.

These playful creatures are sometimes known as the faces of the franchises, and they are definitely parts of their teams.

Four NHL teams have never had a mascot: the Dallas Stars, Edmonton Oilers, New York Rangers, and Philadelphia Flyers.

S.J. SHARKIE OF THE SAN JOSE SHARKS

HARVEY THE HOUND

The first mascot to patrol the stands of an NHL game was the Calgary Flames' dog, Harvey the Hound. Harvey is 6 feet 6 inches (198 cm), weighs 200 pounds (91 kg), and has a long, red tongue hanging from his open mouth. Although mascots usually don't talk, Harvey's tongue has gotten him into some trouble. During a game against the Edmonton Oilers, he started taunting the opposing players from behind the glass. Frustrated Oilers coach Craig MacTavish reached up and ripped the tongue out of the dog's mouth, tossing it into the crowd.

ICEBURGH

Pittsburgh's mascot, a giant Penguin named Iceburgh, is known for making fans smile both during games and outside the arena. The beloved penguin is also a movie star. In 1995 he appeared in the action movie *Sudden Death* with Jean Claude Van Damme.

NORDY

When the Minnesota Wild unveiled its logo in 2000, no one knew what it was. A bear? A cougar? A wolf? Seven years later, the Wild's mascot, Nordy, skated onto the ice for the first time. But the costume didn't clear anything up. All you can say is that he is a wild animal from the north woods with a green "M" on his forehead. He also has a golden mullet—otherwise known as hockey hair—flowing off the back of his neck.

AL THE OCTOPUS

One of the slimiest hockey playoff traditions started in 1952. That's when an octopus was first thrown onto the ice during a Red Wings home playoff game in Detroit. The creature's eight legs represented the eight post-season wins a team needed to capture the Stanley Cup. Although more games are now needed to win the Cup, the tradition continues, and fans still find ways to toss octopuses on the ice. The sea creature is now the Red Wings' unofficial mascot. A giant, inflated purple octopus named Al hangs from the rafters of Joe Louis Arena.

CHAPTER 9
GREATEST MOMENTS

LUCKY NUMBER 7

There are few sporting events as thrilling as a Game 7 of the Stanley Cup Finals. There have been 16 times in NHL history where the championship was decided in Game 7. The latest occurred in 2011, when the Boston Bruins' Patrice Bergeron and Brad Marchand each scored two goals in a shutout of the Vancouver Canucks.

2009 PITTSBURGH PENGUINS

2011 — Bruins 4 — Canucks 0
Goalie Tim Thomas stopped all 37 shots on goal

2009 — Penguins 2 — Red Wings 1
Maxime Talbot scored two goals for Pittsburgh

2006 — Hurricanes 3 — Oilers 1
Rookie goalie Cam Ward won the Conn Smythe Trophy

2004 — Lightning 2 — Flames 1
Ruslan Fedotenko scored both Tampa Bay goals

2003 — Devils 3 — Ducks 0
Goalie Martin Brodeur stopped all 24 shots he faced

2001 — Avalanche 3 — Devils 1
Defenseman Ray Bourque finally won a Cup

2004 TAMPA BAY LIGHTNING

1994 — Rangers 3   Canucks 2
Mark Messier helped New York end a 54-year title drought

1987 — Oilers 3   Flyers 1
Part of Edmonton's dynasty

1971 — Canadiens 3   Blackhawks 2
Rookie goalie Ken Dryden was the playoff MVP

1965 — Canadiens 4   Blackhawks 0
Gump Worsley made 20 saves to shut out Chicago

1964 — Maple Leafs 4   Red Wings 0
Johnny Bower made 33 saves in the shutout

1955 — Red Wings 3   Canadiens 1
Alex Delvecchio scored two goals for the winners

1954 — Red Wings 2   Canadiens 1   OT
The second and most recent Game 7 to go to overtime

1950 — Red Wings 4   Rangers 3   2 OT
The first Game 7 to go to overtime

1945 — Maple Leafs 2   Red Wings 1
Defenseman Babe Pratt scored the game-winning goal

1942 — Maple Leafs 3   Red Wings 1
Toronto erased a 3-games-to-0 deficit in the series

2003 NEW JERSEY DEVILS

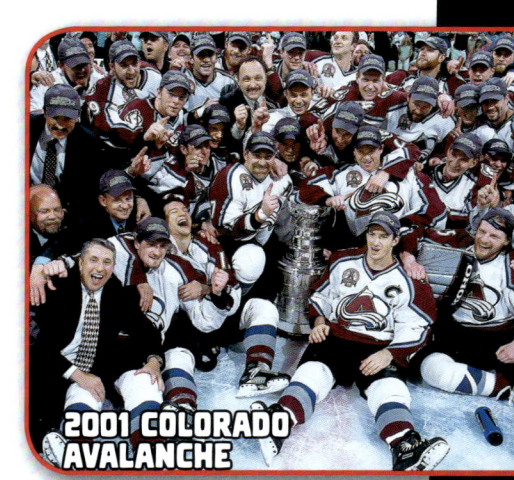
2001 COLORADO AVALANCHE

LONGEST GAMES

One of the reasons playoff hockey games are so exciting is the chance for extended overtime. During the regular season, there is only one overtime before the teams have a shootout. In a shootout, each team has five chances for one of its players to shoot a goal one-on-one with the goalie. The team with the most goals in the shootout wins.

After the regular season ends, shootouts are no longer used to decide a winner. Instead, the games continue until a goal is scored—sudden death. But sometimes the end of the game isn't so sudden. Twice, games have gone into a sixth overtime before someone scores the deciding goal. That's almost the length of two more full games!

WORTH THE WAIT

The longest Stanley Cup-clinching game took place in 1999 when the Dallas Stars beat the Buffalo Sabres 2-1. Brett Hull beat goalie Dominik Hasek with the rebound goal, which came with 5 minutes, 9 seconds remaining in the third overtime.

Date	Score	Game Time	Winning Goal
March 24, 1936	Red Wings 1, Maroons 0	2:56:30	Mud Bruneteau
April 3, 1933	Maple Leafs 1, Bruins 0	2:44:46	Ken Doraty
May 4, 2000	Flyers 2, Penguins 1	2:32:01	Keith Primeau
April 24, 2003	Ducks 4, Stars 3	2:20:48	Petr Sykora
April 24, 1996	Penguins 3, Capitals 2	2:19:15	Petr Nedved
April 11, 2007	Canucks 5, Stars 4	2:18:06	Henrik Sedin
March 23, 1943	Maple Leafs 3, Red Wings 2	2:10:18	Jack McLean
May 4, 2008	Stars 2, Sharks 1	2:09:03	Brenden Morrow
March 28, 1930	Canadiens 2, Rangers 1	2:08:52	Gus Rivers
April 18, 1987	Islanders 3, Capitals 2	2:08:47	Pat LaFontaine

Note: A regular game has 1:00:00 of playing time

Joe Thornton fights for the puck during the May 4, 2008, matchup against the Stars.

GREATEST GOALS

Great plays are made all over the rink during a hockey game. There are incredible saves, pretty passes, and bone-crushing hits. But some of the greatest plays of all are the awe-inspiring goals.

HEXTALL SHOOTS ... AND SCORES?

Philadelphia Flyers goaltender Ron Hextall did a lot more than stop pucks. He was considered one of the best puck-handling and passing goalies in the league. On December 8, 1987, Hextall did something no other goaltender had ever done before—shoot and score a goal. It happened late in the game after the Bruins had pulled their goalie for an extra skater. Hextall stopped the puck and fired it the length of the ice. It was a bull's-eye, right into the empty net. Only nine other goaltenders have scored or been credited with goals in NHL history.

ORR TAKES FLIGHT

Bobby Orr was a defenseman who wasn't afraid to leave the blue line and get in front of the net. It's what made him one of the greatest players of all time. During the 1970 Stanley Cup Finals, Orr won the championship for the Boston Bruins with one of the greatest overtime goals. Orr passed to teammate Derek Sanderson, who was behind the St. Louis Blues' net. Orr then skated down the goal line toward the net. He got the puck back from Sanderson and tapped it into the net before being tripped and flying through the air in celebration.

FACT: In 1979 the New York Islanders' Billy Smith became the first goalie to be credited with a goal. The score happened after the puck bounced off his chest pad and was accidentally shot in the other net by an opposing player. Smith got the credit because he was the last person on his team to touch the puck before it went into the net.

"THE GOAL"

Alex Ovechkin wasn't in the league long before he had a highlight reel that would make veteran players jealous. During his rookie season, he scored what Washington Capitals fans simply refer to as "the goal." After racing down the ice on a rush, Ovechkin appeared to be checked to the ice. He fell to the ice with his back to the goal and his hands above his head. Somehow the future superstar still found a way to shoot the puck past the goalie and into the net.

A LEGG UP

Great goals aren't just scored in the NHL. College players have made jaws drop too. In 1996 University of Michigan forward Mike Legg was alone with the puck behind the University of Minnesota net. He picked up the puck with his stick and tucked it into the upper corner of the goal. It looked more like a lacrosse goal than a hockey goal. The Wolverines went on to beat the Gophers in the NCAA tournament game.

WHICH WAY DID HE GO?

In 2008 Columbus Blue Jackets star forward Rick Nash secured a spot on the list of all-time great goals. He carried the puck into the attacking zone where two defensemen were preparing to stop him. He faked out one defenseman, then another, and then faked out the Coyotes' goaltender before scoring. The goal has been watched on YouTube more than 1 million times.

CHAPTER 10
RINK RECORDS

There's an old saying that records are made to be broken. That might be true, but some records appear to be so out of reach that they'll stay atop their lists forever.

Is it even possible to score a goal faster than two seconds from a center-ice faceoff? Could you imagine a player getting a hat trick in less than 21 seconds? Will we ever see a playoff game inch closer to a seventh overtime than the Detroit Red Wings and the Montreal Maroons did way back in 1936?

We know Wayne Gretzky's records will be difficult to reach, but what about the others? Which ones do you think might be broken someday? Which ones will never be broken?

▼ Canucks vs. Sharks

FASTEST GOALS TO START A GAME

1.	Doug Smail	5 seconds	Jets	1981
	Bryan Trottier	5 seconds	Islanders	1984
	Alexander Mogilny	5 seconds	Sabres	1991
4.	Henry Boucha	6 seconds	Red Wings	1973
	Jean Pronovost	6 seconds	Penguins	1976
	Alex Burrows	6 seconds	Canucks	2013
6.	Charlie Conacher	7 seconds	Maple Leafs	1932
	Danny Gare	7 seconds	Sabres	1978
	Tiger Williams	7 seconds	Kings	1987
	Evgeni Malkin	7 seconds	Penguins	2011

▼ **Bryan Trottier**

LONGEST GAMES

1.	Red Wings 1, Maroons 0	2:56:30	March 24, 1936
2.	Maple Leafs 1, Bruins 0	2:44:46	April 3, 1933
3.	Flyers 2, Penguins 1	2:32:01	May 4, 2000
4.	Ducks 4, Stars 3	2:20:48	April 24, 2003
5.	Penguins 3, Capitals 2	2:19:15	April 24, 1996
6.	Canucks 5, Stars 4	2:18:06	April 11, 2007
7.	Maple Leafs 3, Red Wings 2	2:10:18	March 23, 1943
8.	Stars 2, Sharks 1	2:09:03	May 4, 2008
9.	Canadiens 2, Rangers 1	2:08:52	March 28, 1930
10.	Islanders 3, Capitals 2	2:08:47	April 18, 1987

▲ **Ducks vs. Stars**

RECORD FACT The shortest overtime in playoff history lasted nine seconds. The Montreal Canadiens' Brian Skrudland quickly scored to beat the Calgary Flames on May 18, 1986.

FAST, FASTER, FASTEST

▼ Claude Provost

▼ Claude Provost of the Montreal Canadiens and Denis Savard of the Chicago Blackhawks share the record for the fastest goal to start a period at four seconds.

▼ Nels Stewart of the Montreal Maroons and Deron Quint of the Winnipeg Jets each scored a pair of goals just four seconds apart.

▼ Bill Mosienko of the Blackhawks scored the fastest hat trick in NHL history. In 1952 he scored three goals in a span of 21 seconds.

▼ The fastest a team has scored two goals is three seconds. The Minnesota Wild pulled off the feat in a 2004 game with goals by Jim Dowd and Richard Park. In 1971 the Boston Bruins scored three goals in a record 20 seconds.

▼ Jim Dowd

▼ The St. Louis Blues and the Boston Bruins each scored a goal two seconds apart in 1987. It took only 15 seconds for the Minnesota North Stars and the New York Rangers to score three goals during a game in 1983.

▼ Scoring Streak

Wayne Gretzky started the 1983–84 season with a record 51-game point-scoring streak. The Great One racked up 153 points during the streak. The closest anyone has come to matching it is Mario Lemieux, who scored points in 46 straight games in 1989–90. The longest goal-scoring streak is 16 games set by Punch Broadbent of the Ottawa Senators in 1921–22.

▼ Most Awards

Wayne Gretzky won the Hart Trophy as the NHL's most valuable player a record nine times. The next highest on the list is Gordie Howe, who won the award six times. Bobby Orr won the Norris Trophy as the league's top defenseman eight times. Goaltending great Jacques Plante won the Vezina Trophy as the best goalie seven times.

RECORD FACT Goaltender Tom Barrasso, who played for six teams over 19 seasons, compiled 48 points in his career. Grant Fuhr, who also played goalie for six teams over 19 seasons, had 46 points in his career, including a 14-point season in 1983–84 with the Edmonton Oilers.

▼ Glenn Hall

▼ **Consecutive Games**

When you think of "Ironman" streaks, you think of Cal Ripken Jr. in baseball and Brett Favre in football. But the NHL had an Ironman too. Doug Jarvis played in 964 consecutive games for the Montreal Canadiens, Washington Capitals, and Hartford Whalers between 1975 and 1987.

If there's a record that will never be broken, it may be the consecutive games streak set by goaltender Glenn Hall. The goalie played 502 straight games in goal—551 if you count playoff games. For seven years with the Detroit Red Wings and Chicago Blackhawks, Hall never missed a start— and he played at a time when goalies didn't wear masks! Today most goalies don't play a complete season without giving way to their backups several times.

▼ **Shots and Saves**

The Boston Bruins defeated the Chicago Blackhawks 3-2 on March 4, 1941. But if it wasn't for Chicago goalie Sam LoPresti, the game might have been a blowout. The Bruins put a record 83 shots on goal that day, and LoPresti set a goaltending record by stopping 80 of them.

The most shots on goal recorded in a playoff game was 76 by the Dallas Stars April 11, 2007. Vancouver Canucks goalie Roberto Luongo stopped 72 of them in the four-overtime game and got the 5-4 win.

▲ Roberto Luongo

THE SHOOTOUT

Starting in the 2005–06 season, the NHL adopted a shootout to break ties if neither team scored in overtime of a regular-season game. In the shootout, each team selects three shooters who alternate shooting penalty shots, which are one on one against the goalie. The team with the most shootout goals wins the game.

▼ Vyacheslav Kozlov

MOST SHOOTOUT GOALS (CAREER)			
1.	Brad Boyes	37	Bruins/Blues/Sabres/Islanders/Panthers*
	Zach Parise	37	Devils/Wild*
3.	Mikko Koivu	36	Wild*
4.	Pavel Datsyuk	35	Red Wings*
5.	Radim Vrbata	30	Hurricanes/Blackhawks/Lightning/Coyotes*

*Active player

RECORD FACT Ilya Kovalchuk of the Devils scored 11 shootout goals in 2011–12. Wojtek Wolski of the Avalanche, Jussi Jokinen of the Stars, and Alex Tanguay of the Flames each scored 10 shootout goals in a single season.

SHOOTOUT WINS BY A GOALIE (CAREER)			
1.	Ryan Miller	50	Sabres/Blues*
2.	Henrik Lundqvist	48	Rangers*
3.	Marc-Andre Fleury	45	Penguins*
4.	Martin Brodeur	42	Devils*

*Active player

RECORD FACT Four goaltenders have recorded 10 shootout wins in a single season: the Oilers' Mathieu Garon (2007–08), the Kings' Jonathan Quick (2010–11), and the Devils' Martin Brodeur (2006–07).

▲ Henrik Lundqvist

COACHING WINS

REGULAR SEASON

1.	Scotty Bowman	1,244	Blues/Canadiens/Sabres/Penguins/Red Wings	1967–1980, 1981–1987, 1991–2002
2.	Al Arbour	782	Blues/Islanders	1970–1986, 1988–1994, 2007–2008
3.	Joel Quenneville	706	Blues/Avalanche/Blackhawks	1996–2014*
4.	Dick Irvin	692	Blackhawks/Maple Leafs/Canadiens	1928–1929, 1930–1956
5.	Pat Quinn	684	Flyers/Kings/Canucks/Maple Leafs/Oilers	1978–1982, 1984–1987, 1990–1994, 1995–1996, 1998–2006, 2009–2010
6.	Mike Keenan	672	Flyers/Blackhawks/Rangers/Blues/Canucks/Bruins/Panthers/Flames	1984–1992, 1993–1999, 2000–2004, 2007–2009
7.	Ken Hitchcock	657	Stars/Flyers/Blue Jackets/Blues	1995–2014*
8.	Ron Wilson	648	Ducks/Capitals/Sharks/Maple Leafs	1993–2012
9.	Bryan Murray	620	Capitals/Red Wings/Panthers/Ducks/Senators	1981–1993, 1997–1998, 2001–2002, 2005–2008
10.	Jacques Lemaire	617	Canadiens/Devils/Wild	1983–1985, 1993–1998, 2000–2011

*Active coach

PLAYOFFS

1.	Scotty Bowman	223	Blues/Canadiens/Sabres/Penguins/Red Wings	1967–1980, 1981–1987, 1991–2002
2.	Al Arbour	123	Blues/Islanders	1970–1986, 1988–1994, 2007–2008
3.	Dick Irvin	100	Blackhawks/Maple Leafs/Canadiens	1928–1929, 1930–1956
4.	Joel Quenneville	99	Blues/Avalanch/Blackhawks	1994–2014*
5.	Mike Keenan	96	Flyers/Blackhawks/Rangers/Blues/Canucks/Bruins/Panthers/Flames	1984–1992, 1993–1999, 2000–2004, 2007–2009

COACHING WINS

CHAMPIONSHIPS WON			
1.	Scotty Bowman	9	Canadiens/Penguins/Red Wings
2.	Toe Blake	8	Canadiens
3.	Hap Day	5	Maple Leafs
4.	Al Arbour	4	Islanders
	Punch Imlach	4	Maple Leafs
	Dick Irvin	4	Maple Leafs/Canadiens
	Glen Sather	4	Oilers

AMERICAN RECORDS

Most of the top record-breakers in NHL history hail from Canada. But there are exceptions. Jari Kurri is from Finland, Jaromir Jagr is from the Czech Republic, and Evgeni Nabokov is from Russia. What about players from the United States? Here are some of the American records:

CAREER GOALS

Mike Modano	561	North Stars/Stars/Red Wings	1989–2011

CAREER ASSISTS

Phil Housley	894	Sabres/Jets/Blues/Flames/Devils/Capitals/Blackhawks/Maple Leafs	1982–2003

CAREER POINTS

Mike Modano	1,374	North Stars/Stars/Red Wings	1989–2011

CAREER GOALIE WINS

John Vanbiesbrouck	374	Rangers/Panthers/Flyers/Islanders/Devils	1981–1982, 1983–2002

CAREER SHUTOUTS

Frank Brimsek	40	Bruins/Blackhawks	1938–1943, 1945–1950

▼ Mike Modano

TIMELINE

1873	The rules of hockey are first written by James Creighton in Montreal
1877	The first organized hockey team is formed at McGill University in Montreal
1891	The first women's hockey games are played
1893	The first Stanley Cup games are played
1909	The Montreal Canadiens are founded
1917	The National Hockey League is formed; the Seattle Metropolitans of the Pacific Coast Hockey Association become the first American team to win the Stanley Cup
1920	Men's hockey is played in the Olympics for the first time; Canada takes the gold medal in Antwerp, Belgium
1924	The Boston Bruins play in the first NHL game in the United States
1942	The Brooklyn Americans (formerly the New York Americans) fold, leaving the NHL with its Original Six teams
1948	The University of Michigan wins the first NCAA men's hockey championship
1967	The NHL expands to 12 teams
1972	The new professional league called the World Hockey Association is formed; several NHL stars, including Chicago's Bobby Hull, jump to the new league
1978	Wayne Gretzky makes his professional debut with the Indianapolis Racers of the WHA; eight games into the season he was traded to Edmonton
1979	The WHA's remaining teams—the Edmonton Oilers, Quebec Nordiques, Hartford Whalers, and the Winnipeg Jets—merge into the NHL

1980	The United States pulls off the "Miracle on Ice" during the Olympics, upsetting the mighty Soviet Union
1998	NHL players compete in the Olympics; women's hockey is played in the Olympics for the first time
1999	Wayne Gretzky retires as the NHL's all-time leading scorer
2004	The NHL season doesn't start because of a disagreement between team owners and players; the season is canceled and, for the first time since 1919, the Stanley Cup was not awarded
2005	Shootouts after overtimes are introduced to regular-season NHL games, meaning there are no more tie games
2010	Sidney Crosby scores the game-winning goal in overtime as Canada defeats the United States 3-2 in the men's gold medal game of the Winter Olympics in Vancouver
2014	The Los Angeles KIngs capture their second Stanley Cup in a three-year span, defeating the New York Rangers 4 games to 1.

Match the current NHL team with its original home.

Carolina Hurricanes	Inglewood, California
Dallas Stars	Landover, Maryland
Arizona Coyotes	Quebec City, Quebec, Canada
Washington Capitals	San Francisco, California
Calgary Flames	Atlanta, Georgia
New Jersey Devils	Winnipeg, Manitoba, Canada
Colorado Avalanche	Boston, Massachusetts
San Jose Sharks	Bloomington, Minnesota
Los Angeles Kings	Kansas City, Missouri

Answer: Hurricanes—Boston; Stars—Bloomington; Coyotes—Winnipeg; Capitals—Landover; Flames—Atlanta; Devils—Kansas City; Avalanche—Quebec City; Sharks—San Francisco; Kings—Inglewood

READ MORE

Frederick, Shane. *The Technology of Hockey.*
North Mankato, Minn.: Capstone Press, 2013.

Frederick Shane et al. *The Ultimate Guide to Pro Hockey Teams 2015.*
North Mankato, Minn: Capstone Press, 2012.

Gitlin, Martin. *The Stanley Cup: All about Pro Hockey's Biggest Event.*
North Mankato, Minn: Capstone Press, 2012.

Morrison, Jessica. *Wayne Gretzky: Greatness on Ice.*
New York: Crabtree Publishing, 2011.

INTERNET SITES

FactHound offers a safe, fun way to find Internet sites related to this book. All of the sites on FactHound have been researched by our staff.

Here's all you do:

Visit www.facthound.com

Type in this code: 9781491419625

INDEX

Anderson, Craig, 45, 46
Anderson, Glenn, 77, 85, 88, 89, 90
Andreychuk, Dave, 22, 37
Arbour, Al, 74, 78, 79, 101, 122, 123
Arnott, Jason, 95

Babando, Pete, 87
Backstrom, Niklas, 45
Barber, Bill, 86
Barrasso, Tom, 44, 46, 90, 119
Baxter, Paul, 35
Belfour, Ed, 41, 46, 47, 48, 90, 91, 94, 95
Beliveau, Jean, 51, 59, 61, 84, 85, 91, 98
Benedict, Clint, 43, 92
Berube, Craig, 35
Billington, Craig, 44
Bladon, Tom, 34
Blake, Toe, 79, 123
Bondra, Peter, 25
Bossy, Mike, 26, 27, 60, 70, 85, 86, 87, 89
Boston Bruins, 20, 21, 30, 36, 42, 58, 67, 68, 69, 70, 71, 72, 76, 77, 83, 84, 96, 101, 104, 108, 111, 112, 117, 118, 120, 124
Boucha, Henry, 117
Boucher, Brian, 47
Bourque, Ray, 18, 28, 30, 31, 32, 33, 37, 53, 61, 88, 108
Bowman, Scotty, 77, 78, 79, 98, 122, 123
Boyes, Brad, 121
Brashear, Donald, 35
Brimsek, Frank, 101, 123
Broadbent, Punch, 119
Broda, Turk, 55, 92, 94
Brodeur, Martin, 40, 41, 42, 43, 44, 46, 47, 48, 49, 54, 55, 61, 63, 90, 91, 94, 95, 108, 121
Broten, Neal, 27, 103
Bryzgalov, Ilya, 93
Buffalo Sabres, 59, 69, 70, 84, 104, 110
Bure, Pavel, 25, 26, 27, 101
Burke, Sean, 46
Byfuglien, Dustin, 87

Calgary Flames, 23, 49, 68, 71, 72, 97, 106, 108, 117, 121, 125
Carbonneau, Guy, 90
Chabot, Lorne, 43, 92
Cheevers, Gerry, 42
Chelios, Chris, 30, 32, 36, 37, 52, 53, 60, 90
Chicago Blackhawks, 67, 68, 69, 70, 71, 72, 83, 84, 87, 96, 97, 109, 118, 120
Ciccarelli, Dino, 22
Clancy, King, 75, 99
Clarke, Bobby, 33, 34, 59
Clarkson Golden Knights, 103
Coffey, Paul, 24, 28, 30, 31, 32, 34, 53, 77, 88, 89, 105
Conacher, Charlie, 117
Connell, Alec, 43, 47, 48, 92
Cournoyer, Yvan, 84
Crosby, Sidney, 27, 56, 59, 63, 100, 102, 125

Dallas Stars, 71, 72, 84, 87, 106, 110, 111, 117, 120, 121, 125
Datsyuk, Pavel, 121
Day, Hap, 79, 123
Delvecchio, Alex, 36, 109
Denis, Marc, 46
Denneny, Cy, 26
Detroit Red Wings, 14, 19, 29, 36, 37, 67, 69, 70, 72, 77, 78, 83, 84, 87, 96, 97, 107, 108, 109, 111, 116, 117, 120
Dionne, Marcel, 19, 21, 22, 24, 26, 28, 94
Dolson, Dolly, 43
Domi, Tie, 35
Doraty, Ken, 111
Doughty, Drew, 57
Dowd, Jim, 118
Draper, Kris, 90
Druce, John, 86
Dryden, Ken, 43, 55, 75, 91, 94, 109

Edmonton Oilers, 18, 19, 29, 34, 58, 66, 67, 68, 69, 71, 72, 75, 77, 79, 83, 88, 94, 106, 108, 109, 119, 124
Elias, Patrik, 24
Elliott, Brian, 45

Esposito, Phil, 19, 21, 22, 25, 26, 59
Esposito, Tony, 41, 44, 47, 48

Fedorov, Sergei, 23, 24, 25, 77, 88
Fleury, Theoren, 23
Francis, Ron, 19, 28, 37
Franzen, Johan, 87, 101
Fuhr, Grant, 41, 44, 46, 47, 90, 91, 105, 119

Gardiner, Charlie, 43
Gare, Danny, 69, 117
Gartner, Mike, 21, 22
Giguere, Jean-Sebastien, 93, 95
Gilbert, Gilles, 42
Gilmour, Doug, 88, 89
Goring, Butch, 23
Goulet, Michel, 22, 25
Graham, Dirk, 23, 24
Gretzky, Wayne, 18, 19, 20, 21, 23, 24, 26, 27, 28, 29, 33, 34, 50, 51, 58, 59, 60, 61, 63, 68, 71, 75, 77, 85, 86, 87, 88, 89, 100, 105, 119, 124, 125

Hainsworth, George, 40, 43, 48, 55, 92
Halak, Jaraslav, 45
Hall, Glenn, 41, 47, 48, 120
Hamilton Tigers, 69
Hanlon, Glen, 93
Hartford Whalers, 69, 70, 120, 124
Hasek, Dominik, 43, 45, 46, 48, 55, 59, 90, 92, 93, 94, 95, 110
Hatcher, Kevin, 31
Hawerchuk, Dale, 27, 29
Henning, Lorne, 86
Hextall, Ron, 49, 112
Hiller, Jonas, 45, 93
Hitchcock, Ken, 122
Holt, Randy, 36
Horton, Tim, 36
Housley, Phil, 30, 31, 32, 84, 123
Howard, Jimmy, 45
Howe, Gordie, 18, 19, 21, 28, 36, 37, 50, 51, 59, 60, 62, 100, 119

Howe, Mark, 34
Hrudey, Kelly, 93
Hull, Bobby, 26, 42, 51, 59, 60, 62, 100, 124
Hull, Brett, 21, 22, 24, 25, 26, 60, 85, 87, 89, 110
Hunter, Dale, 35
Hunter, Tim, 35

Imlach, Punch, 79, 123
Irvin, Dick, 79, 122, 123

Jagr, Jaromir, 19, 21, 24, 25, 88, 89, 123
Jarvis, Doug, 120
Jokinen, Jussi, 121
Jokinen, Olli, 24
Joseph, Curtis, 41, 44, 46, 47, 90, 94
Juneau, Joe, 27

Kane, Patrick, 57, 87
Kansas City Scouts, 67, 70
Keenan, Mike, 79, 122
Kelly, Red, 31, 53, 84
Kerr, Dave, 43, 92
Kerr, Tim, 18, 22, 86
Khabibulin, Nikolai, 46, 95
Kiprusoff, Miikka, 42, 45, 93, 95
Kocur, Joe, 35
Kolzig, Olaf, 93
Kovalchuk, Ilya, 24, 121
Krupp, Uwe, 87
Kurri, Jari, 21, 23, 25, 26, 77, 85, 87, 88, 89, 123

LA Kings, 125
Lafleur, Guy, 25, 33, 34, 51, 59, 76
Lalime, Patrick, 92, 93
Lalonde, Newsy, 86
Larmer, Steve, 27
Leach, Reggie, 85, 86
Lecavalier, Vincent, 26
Leetch, Brian, 30, 31, 32
Leinonen, Mikko, 88
Lemaire, Jacques, 84, 122
Lemieux, Claude, 85, 90
Lemieux, Mario, 19, 20, 21, 22, 23, 24, 26, 27, 29, 51, 58, 59, 61, 70, 86, 87, 88, 89, 105, 119

Leswick, Tony, 87
Lidstrom, Nicklas, 30, 31, 32, 33, 37, 53, 61, 88, 90
Liut, Mike, 44
LoPresti, Sam, 120
Los Angeles Kings, 36, 58, 68, 71, 72, 75, 94, 125
Lumley, Harry, 44
Lundqvist, Henrik, 43, 45, 93, 121
Luongo, Roberto, 40, 42, 45, 46, 54, 120

MacInnis, Al, 30, 31, 32, 88
Malkin, Evgeni, 57, 89, 117
Malone, Joe, 20, 24
Marchand, Brad, 108
Marchant, Todd, 86
Martin, Rick, 27
Martinez, Alec, 87
Mason, Chris, 49, 104
McAuley, Ken, 44
McCrimmon, Brad, 34
McNeil, Gerry, 92
McRae, Basil, 35
McSorley, Marty, 35
Meloche, Gilles, 44
Messier, Mark, 18, 19, 21, 23, 28, 29, 36, 37, 51, 59, 61, 77, 85, 88, 89, 90, 105, 109
Mikkelson, Bill, 34
Millen, Greg, 44
Miller, Ryan, 57, 103, 104, 121
Minnesota North Stars, 69, 118
Minnesota Wild, 71, 96, 107, 118
Modano, Mike, 71, 123
Mogilny, Alexander, 21, 117
Montreal Canadiens, 12, 14, 24, 53, 54, 55, 59, 67, 68, 69, 70, 72, 75, 76, 77, 78, 79, 83, 84, 91, 96, 97, 98, 100, 109, 111, 117, 118, 120, 124
Montreal Maroons, 73, 111, 116, 117, 118
Montreal Shamrocks, 73
Montreal Wanderers, 69, 73, 98
Moog, Andy, 90, 91
Mosienko, Bill, 118
Murphy, Larry, 30, 31, 32, 37
Murray, Bryan, 122

Nabokov, Evgeni, 40, 42, 49, 104, 123

Narlsson, Erik, 57
Neely, Cam, 25, 86
New Jersey Devils, 40, 54, 70, 71, 72, 83, 89, 95, 108, 121, 125
New York Islanders, 15, 20, 37, 67, 68, 70, 72, 74, 78, 79, 83, 96, 111, 112, 117
New York Rangers, 14, 15, 69, 70, 72, 83, 84, 87, 88, 96, 104, 106, 109, 111, 117, 118
Niedermayer, Scott, 24, 52
Nieuwendyk, Joe, 22, 25, 27, 87
Nilan, Chris, 35, 36
Nilsson, Kent, 24
Noronen, Mika, 49

Oates, Adam, 28
Orr, Bobby, 30, 31, 32, 33, 34, 52, 53, 59, 61, 63, 112, 119
Osgood, Chris, 41, 49, 90, 91, 94
Ottawa Senators, 37, 47, 67, 69, 70, 73, 75, 119
Ovechkin, Alex, 24, 27, 56, 59, 60, 62, 113

Parent, Bernie, 42
Park, Richard, 118
Payne, Steve, 85
Pederson, Barry, 27
Peluso, Mike, 35
Philadelphia Flyers, 14, 34, 37, 68, 70, 72, 84, 87, 94, 97, 101, 106, 109, 111, 112, 117
Pisani, Fernando, 87
Pittsburgh Penguins, 12, 14, 51, 56, 66, 67, 68, 69, 70, 72, 78, 83, 89, 94, 96, 102, 107, 108, 111, 117
Plante, Jacques, 12, 41, 48, 55, 59, 91, 94, 119
Potvin, Denis, 30, 31, 32, 33, 53, 61
Potvin, Felix, 46
Poulin, Dave, 23
Poilun, Marie-Philip, 103
Pratt, Babe, 32, 109
Presley, Wayne, 86
Price, Carey, 45
Probert, Bob, 35
Pronovost, Jean, 117
Propp, Brian, 86
Provost, Claude, 84, 118
Quebec Bulldogs, 20, 69, 73
Quebec Nordiques, 67, 69, 71, 124
Quenneville, Joel, 122
Quick, Jonathan, 57, 93
Quinn, Pat, 122
Quint, Deron, 118

Ranford, Bill, 46
Rask, Tukka, 93
Ray, Rob, 35
Recchi, Mark, 37, 88, 101
Reese, Jeff, 49
Rhodes, Damian, 49
Richard, Henri, 84, 91, 98
Richard, Maurice, 26, 51, 60, 84, 85, 86, 100
Richards, Brad, 82, 87
Rinne, Pekka, 45
Roach, John Ross, 43, 92
Robinson, Larry, 30, 32, 33, 34, 53, 90
Robitaille, Luc, 22, 27, 60
Roenick, Jeremy, 25
Roloson, Dwayne, 45
Rolston, Brian, 24
Roy, Patrick, 41, 44, 46, 47, 54, 55, 61, 82, 90, 91, 94

Sakic, Joe, 19, 26, 85, 87, 89
Sanderson, Derek, 86, 112
San Jose Sharks, 49, 58, 67, 68, 69, 71, 104, 106, 111, 117, 125
Sather, Glen, 79, 123
Savard, Denis, 118
Savard, Serge, 33, 84
Sawchuk, Terry, 40, 41, 42, 44, 47, 48, 55, 61, 63, 92, 94
Schneider, Corey, 45
Schultz, Dave, 35, 101
Selanne, Teemu, 21, 25, 27, 101
Shanahan, Brendan, 22, 24, 25
Shutt, Steve, 34, 76
Sidorkiewicz, Peter, 44
Sillinger, Mike, 37
Sittler, Darryl, 20, 86
Skrudland, Brian, 117
Smail, Doug, 117
Smith, Billy, 49, 90, 91, 112
Smith, Bobby, 87
Smith, Dallas, 34
Smith, Gary, 41, 44
Stackhouse, Ron, 32
Stapleton, Pat, 32
Stastny, Peter, 27

Stevens, Kevin, 85
Stevens, Scott, 37, 90
Stewart, Nels, 59, 118
St. Louis Blues, 14, 37, 71, 84, 112, 118
Sundin, Mats, 24, 25, 26
Sundstrom, Patrik, 89
Suter, Gary, 32

Talbot, Jean-Guy, 84
Tanguay, Alex, 121
Tavares, John, 57
Taylor, Billy, 29
Theodore, Jose, 49, 59
Thomas, Tim, 45, 93, 108
Thompson, Tiny, 43, 48, 92
Tocchet, Rick, 35
Toronto Arenas, 69, 70
Toronto Maple Leafs, 20, 31, 69, 70, 72, 74, 79, 83, 84, 96, 109, 111, 117
Toronto St. Patricks, 69, 70
Trottier, Bryan, 20, 27, 33, 74, 117
Tugnutt, Ron, 93
Turco, Marty, 45, 93, 121
Turnbull, Ian, 31

Union Dutchmen, 103

Vanbiesbrouck, John, 44, 46, 47, 123
Vancouver Canucks, 15, 37, 57, 69, 71, 108, 109, 111, 117, 120
Vernon, Mike, 90, 91
Vokoun, Tomas, 45, 46
Vyborny, David, 26

Ward, Cam, 46, 49, 99, 108
Washington Capitals, 67, 68, 69, 70, 84, 111, 113, 117, 120, 125
Williams, Tiger, 35, 117
Wilson, Doug, 31
Wilson, Ron, 122
Winkler, Hal, 48
Winnipeg Jets, 29, 67, 68, 69, 71, 118, 124
Wolski, Wojtek, 121
Worsley, Gump, 41, 44, 47, 109
Worters, Roy, 43, 59

Yzerman, Steve, 19, 21, 23, 25, 28, 77, 89

Ultimate Guide to PRO HOCKEY TEAMS 2015

by Shane Frederick,
Luke DeCock, and
Martin Gitlin

capstone
young readers

Sports Illustrated Kids The Ultimate Guide to Pro Hockey Teams 2015 is published by Capstone Young Readers, 1710 Roe Crest Drive, North Mankato, MN 56003. www.capstonepub.com

Copyright © 2015 by Capstone Young Readers, a Capstone imprint. All rights reserved.

No part of this publication may be reproduced in whole or in part, or stored in a retrieval system, or transmitted in any form or by any means, electronic, mechanical, photocopying, recording, or otherwise, without written permission of the publisher.

Sports Illustrated Kids is a trademark of Time Inc. Used with permission.

For information regarding permission, write to Capstone Young Readers, 1710 Roe Crest Drive, North Mankato, Minnesota 56003.

Library of Congress Cataloging-in-Publication Data
Cataloging-in-publication information is on file with the Library of Congress.
ISBN 978-1-4914-1963-2

Edited by Clare Lewis and Anthony Wacholtz
Designed by Richard Parker and Eric Manske
Media Research by Eric Gohl
Production by Helen McCreath

Image Credits:
AP Photo: 74, A.E. Maloof, 29, Tom Pidgeon, 101; BigStockPhoto.com: Christopher Penler, 80t; Corbis: Bettmann, 26, 52, 56, 68, 71, 82, 85; Getty Images: Allsport/Robert Laberge, 91, Bruce Bennett Studios, 6, 17, 31t, 50, 69, 72, 73, 83, 89, 100, 103, Focus On Sport, 37t, 58, 90, Hulton Archive, 112, NHL Images/Allsport/Glenn Cratty, 61b, NY Daily News Archive/Keith Torrie, 19, Pictorial Parade, 113; iStockphotos: Mark Stay, 120–121, Stefan Klein, 120 (puck); Newscom: 87b, 97t, 109t, AFP/Dan Levine, 107b, Icon SMI/Jason Cohn, 117t, Icon SMI/Jason Mowry, 45t, Icon SMI/Robert Beck, 59, Icon SMI/Shelly Castellano, 33b, Icon SMI/Southcreek Sports/Adrian Gauthier, 110b, Images Distribution, 111b, Reuters/Gary Caskey, 40, Reuters/Mike Segar, 43, Reuters/STR, 8, UPI Photo/John Dickerson, 61t, Zuma Press/The Sporting News, 37b; Sports Illustrated: Bob Rosato, 86b, 108t, 108b, 111t, 119b, Damian Strohmeyer, 24t, 79t, 93t, 98b, 110t, 118b, 123, David E. Klutho, cover, 1, 4–5, 7, 9, 20, 22t, 22b, 23t, 23b, 24b, 30t, 30b, 31b, 32t, 32b, 33t, 34t, 34b, 35b, 36t, 36b, 38t, 38b, 39t, 39b, 42, 44t, 44b, 45b, 46t, 46b, 47b, 48t, 49t, 49b, 54t, 54b, 55b, 60t, 60b, 62b, 63t, 64t, 64b, 65t, 65b, 66t, 76t, 76b, 77t, 77b, 78t, 78b, 79b, 92t, 92b, 93b, 94t, 94b, 96t, 98t, 99t, 99b, 104t, 104b, 109b, 114t, 114b, 115t, 115b, 118t, Heinz Kluetmeier, 15, Hy Peskin, 10, 11, 48b, 51, 66b, 67b, John D. Hanlon, 25b, 28, 95t, 95b, John G. Zimmerman, 86t, John Iacono, 13, 80b, John W. McDonough, 62t, Manny Millan, 12, 35t, 81t, 81b, Robert Beck, 21, 47t, 63b, 96b, 97b, 105t, 105b, 106t, 106b, 107t, 116b, 117b, 122, Simon Bruty, 116t, 119t, Tony Triolo, 2, 25t, 55t, 67t, V.J. Lovero, 87t

Design Elements: iStockphotos, Shutterstock

Printed in Canada.
092014   007105

TABLE OF CONTENTS

The Greatest Show on Ice 4
The Stanley Cup 6
Greatest Dynasties 10
Amazing Moments 16
Anaheim Ducks 22
Arizona Coyotes 24
Boston Bruins 26
Buffalo Sabres 32
Calgary Flames 34
Carolina Hurricanes 36
Chicago Blackhawks 38
Colorado Avalanche 40
Columbus Blue Jackets 46
Dallas Stars 48
Detroit Red Wings 50
Edmonton Oilers 56
Florida Panthers 62
Los Angeles Kings 64
Minnesota Wild 66
Montreal Canadiens 68

Nashville Predators 78
New Jersey Devils 80
New York Islanders 82
New York Rangers 88
Ottawa Senators 94
Philadelphia Flyers 96
Pittsburgh Penguins 98
San Jose Sharks 104
St. Louis Blues 106
Tampa Bay Lightning 108
Toronto Maple Leafs 110
Vancouver Canucks 114
Washington Capitals 116
Winnipeg Jets 118
Team Map 120
1960–2014 Stanley Cup Winners 122
Glossary 124
Read More 126
Internet Sites 126
Index 127

THE GREATEST SHOW ON ICE

From its origins on the frozen ponds of Canada to the crowded arenas of today, the game of hockey has always had many loyal fans who cheer every goal, assist, and crunching body check. Hockey is now popular from coast to coast and all the way from Canada to the southern United States. Fans now pack huge arenas every year to cheer for their favorite team.

Today, professional hockey is a much faster and bigger sport than it once was. The NHL now has 30 teams, which this book will explore in detail, looking at both the history and the present-day achievements of each team.

A RICH HISTORY

But as much as fans enjoy the excitement of watching a game, they also enjoy being part of a game that has a century of history. For many years, there were only six teams in the National Hockey League (NHL). These teams are known as the "Original Six" (see the box). It was a slower and rougher game then, but it was full of stories.

The Original Six

The "Original Six" teams in the NHL were the Boston Bruins, Chicago Black Hawks, Detroit Red Wings, Montreal Canadiens, New York Rangers, and Toronto Maple Leafs.

GREAT TEAMS AND STARS

This book also features in-depth looks at some of hockey's greatest individual championship teams and stars. Gordie Howe, Wayne Gretzky, Mario Lemieux, and Bobby Orr, the four greatest players in hockey history, all played on championship teams. New stars are also leading great teams today.

THE STANLEY CUP

The Stanley Cup is the oldest and most famous trophy in professional sports. It has become the symbol of the NHL. Each season, every team sets a goal of winning the Cup.

THE HISTORY OF THE CUP

In 1893 the Montreal Amateur Athletics Association captured the Amateur Hockey Association's championship. Its prize for winning was a $50 silver bowl donated by Sir Frederick Arthur Stanley, the governor general of Canada.

The Montreal Amateur Athletics Association won the first Stanley Cup title in 1893.

After this, the Cup became the trophy teams played for in the "Challenge Cup Era." From 1893 to 1913, Canadian hockey clubs challenged each other to determine the Stanley Cup champion.

Then, from 1914 to 1917, the champions of the Pacific Coast Hockey Association (PCHA) and National Hockey Association (NHA) played for the Stanley Cup. But during these years, many of the NHA's top players left to fight in World War I (1914–1918). With a lack of quality players, the NHA broke apart in 1917.

Several NHA franchise owners soon formed the NHL. The league named the annual championship the Stanley Cup finals. The Cup itself became the prize for winning the title. And today, it keeps getting bigger. More rings are added to the base of the Cup as it is filled with the names of winning players each year.

Winning the Stanley Cup is always cause for great celebration!

THE NHL SEASON AND PLAYOFFS

Today, each of the 30 NHL teams starts each season with the dream of winning the Stanley Cup. The teams are split into the Eastern Conference and Western Conference. Each conference has two divisions of seven or eight teams. Teams play 82 games during the regular season. They receive two points for each victory. If they lose, they get zero points. If a team loses in overtime or in a shootout loss, they receive one point. Overtimes and shootouts are played when teams end three regular periods of play in a tie.

The top eight teams in each conference reach the playoffs. The top three teams from each division advance to the post-season, as do the conference's next two best teams, called wild card teams.

Each playoff round consists of a best-of-seven series. The teams battle through three rounds of playoffs to determine the Eastern and Western Conference winners. The conference champions then play each other in the Stanley Cup finals. The first team to win four games in the finals series is declared the NHL champion.

Fun with the Cup

After the Stanley Cup finals, each player from the winning team gets to keep the Cup for one day during the offseason. The trophy has been on boat rides, in parades, and at parties all around the world! Over the years the Cup has been used as everything from a flowerpot to a soup bowl. It has been used to baptize babies. And some players have allowed their pets to drink out of it!

During a trip to his home country of Slovakia, Detroit's Tomas Kopecky ate tripe soup out of the Stanley Cup!

GREATEST DYNASTIES

Throughout Stanley Cup history, several teams have been powerhouses. They've played in many championship series and have come away with several titles. But a few teams have risen even higher to become true dynasties in the league. (For more on these individual teams, read their chapters and "Great Teams in Focus" panels throughout this book.)

Most Stanley Cup Championships

Montreal Canadiens	24
Toronto Maple Leafs	13
Detroit Red Wings	11
Boston Bruins	6
Edmonton Oilers	5

Montreal Canadiens wing Maurice "Rocket" Richard

CANADA IN COMMAND

From 1942 through most of the 1960s, the Stanley Cup rarely traveled outside of Canada. The Montreal Canadiens and Toronto Maple Leafs dominated the Cup. The Canadiens won 18 titles from 1944 to 1979.

During those 36 seasons, Montreal reached the finals an amazing 24 times. When the Canadiens didn't win the Stanley Cup, the Maple Leafs usually did. The team captured 6 out of 10 titles from 1942 to 1951. Toronto went on to win four more championships between 1962 and 1967.

Montreal Canadiens goalie Gerry McNeil

Montreal Canadiens defenseman Emile "Butch" Bouchard

SUPER ISLANDERS

The NHL began adding teams and expanded rapidly in the late 1960s. It soon became nearly impossible for one team to dominate the Stanley Cup. One exception was the New York Islanders, the first U.S. team to enjoy a dynasty.

The Islanders first entered the league in 1972. They snagged their first Stanley Cup just eight years later, in 1980. The team went on to win three more championships from 1981 to 1983.

The Islanders featured several future NHL Hall of Famers, including Mike Bossy and Bryan Trottier. During their four-year dynasty, the Islanders compiled an incredible 16–3 record in the Stanley Cup finals. During the 1982 and 1983 finals, they never lost a game.

The defensive play of wing Bob Nystrom (opposite) and offensive skills of center Bryan Trottier were key parts of the New York Islanders' championship years.

OVERPOWERING OILERS

The Islanders' dynasty ended just as the Edmonton Oilers began their own. Some believe the Oilers were the most explosive team in NHL history. The team began showing their dominance in 1984. They overpowered their opponents while averaging a league-record 5.58 goals per game. They won the Stanley Cup that year, and again in 1985, 1987, 1988, and 1990.

The Oilers didn't just steamroll through the regular season and playoffs every year. They dominated the championship round, too. With superstar center Wayne Gretzky leading the way, the Oilers scored an average of 21 goals in all five Stanley Cup titles.

The Oilers defense was also dominant during the team's championship years. Opponents averaged just 2.4 goals per game in those series. In the 1990 finals, the Oilers held the Boston Bruins to just eight goals in five games.

Most Points Scored in a Stanley Cup Final Series

Points	Player, Team	Opponent	Year
13	Wayne Gretzky, Oilers	Bruins	1988
12	Gordie Howe, Red Wings	Canadiens	1955
12	Yvan Cournoyer, Canadiens	Blackhawks	1973
12	Jacques Lemaire, Canadiens	Blackhawks	1973
12	Mario Lemieux, Penguins	North Stars	1991

Wayne Gretzky won the 1985 Stanley Cup Most Valuable Player (MVP) award while leading Edmonton to its second championship.

AMAZING MOMENTS

The Stanley Cup finals are often filled with excitement and drama. Over the years the finals have had some historic moments.

1987: EDMONTON VS. PHILADELPHIA

In the 1986–1987 season, the Philadelphia Flyers had the second-best defense in the NHL. The Edmonton Oilers had the NHL's finest offense. It was only a matter of time before the two teams battled for the Stanley Cup championship.

Edmonton won three of the first four games, and Oilers fans were already boasting about a victory parade. But the Flyers showed their talent and guts. The team fell behind by two goals in both Games 5 and 6. But they stormed back to win both games and force a Game 7.

However, Edmonton proved to be too strong of a team. Goaltender Grant Fuhr shut down the Flyers in a 3–1 victory in Game 7. The Oilers won their third championship in four years, and the fans got to enjoy their victory parade.

The Oilers' Mark Messier (left) and the Flyers' Dave Poulin battled to control the puck during Game 3 of the 1987 Stanley Cup finals.

1942: TORONTO VS. DETROIT

The Toronto Maple Leafs appeared doomed in the 1942 Stanley Cup finals. They lost the first two games at home against the Detroit Red Wings. Then they lost Game 3 in Detroit as well.

Toronto coach Hap Day decided to take drastic action. He benched several veteran players and replaced them with rookies. Led by future Hall of Famer Syl Apps, the Leafs responded with three straight wins to force the first Game 7 in Stanley Cup history. In the final game, Toronto's goaltender Turk Broda kept the Red Wings to just one goal. The Leafs won the final game 3–1, achieving possibly the greatest comeback in NHL history.

1994: VANCOUVER VS. NEW YORK

The last time the New York Rangers had won the Stanley Cup, the NHL had just six teams. But the Rangers' fortunes were about to change in the 1994 Stanley Cup finals. The Rangers won three of the first four games against the Vancouver Canucks. New York was on the brink of winning its first championship in 54 years. But the Canucks stormed back to tie the series.

Game 7 and the title were decided at Madison Square Garden in front of nearly 20,000 fans. The fans would not go home disappointed. Star forward Mark Messier scored a goal and an assist to lead the Rangers to a 3–2 victory. After more than 50 years, the Rangers had finally captured another Stanley Cup title. (For more on this amazing championship battle, see pages 88 to 91.)

New York fans celebrated the Rangers' Stanley Cup title with a ticker-tape parade.

LOPSIDED SHOCKER

The Vancouver Canucks were expected to win it all in 2011. The team had the most explosive offense and the strongest defense in the NHL. Vancouver had won 8 of 11 games leading up to the championship round.

But the Canucks seemed outmatched by Boston in the 2011 Stanley Cup series. Vancouver earned a narrow 1–0 victory in the first game of the series. Game 2 went to overtime, which the Canucks also won 3–2.

But then the Bruins turned up the heat. Boston's offense exploded to score 21 goals over the five games and claim the title. Meanwhile, the Canucks managed to score only four goals. Although they were favored to win the championship, Vancouver couldn't overcome Boston's powerful offense.

Boston finished the series with 15 more goals than Vancouver. The Canucks set a record low by scoring just eight goals in seven games. It was the most lopsided score ever seen in a seven-game Stanley Cup series.

Boston Bruins defenseman Zdeno Chara

Boston Bruins wing Michael Ryder

Vancouver Canucks goalie Roberto Luongo

ANAHEIM DUCKS

Franchise Record: 722–637–107–108
Home Rink: Honda Center (17,174 capacity) in Anaheim, California

STANLEY CUP
2007

First Season: 1993–1994

The Anaheim Ducks were all Hollywood when they joined the NHL. They were owned by the Walt Disney Company. They got their name—then called the Mighty Ducks of Anaheim—from a popular Disney hockey movie. The goalie even wore a mask that featured the face of cartoon character Donald Duck. But they are no joke. The Ducks have twice gone to the Stanley Cup finals and won it all in 2007.

2007 Stanley Cup celebration

Franchise records are listed by wins, losses, ties, and overtime losses.

Legends & Stars

Teemu Selanne

Paul Kariya	LW	1994–2003	Two-time Lady Byng Trophy winner
Scott Niedermayer	D	2005–2010	Longtime New Jersey Devil was a Conn Smythe winner with the Ducks
Corey Perry	RW	2005–2014	Led NHL in goals and won Hart Trophy in 2011
Teemu Selanne	RW	1996–2001, 2005–2014	NHL's goal leader in 1999 has played in 10 All-Star Games

By the Numbers

TOP GOAL SCORER
Teemu Selanne
1996–2001,
2005–2014
448 goals

TOP ASSISTS MAN
Teemu Selanne
457 goals
531 assists

TOP GOALTENDER
Jean-Sebastien Giguere
2000–2010
206 wins

TOP DEFENSEMAN
Scott Niedermayer
2005–2010
264 points

All regular season stats are through the 2013–14 season.

Consolation Prize

The Conn Smythe Trophy is awarded to the MVP of the Stanley Cup playoffs every year. A player on the losing team of the finals has won the award only five times in NHL history. Ducks goaltender Jean-Sebastien Giguere was one of those players. Although the Ducks fell to the Devils in Game 7 of the 2003 finals, Giguere's five shutouts in the playoffs earned him the award.

Sibling Rivalry

Rob Niedermayer watched his older brother, Scott, lift the Stanley Cup with the New Jersey Devils three times. Rob never touched the trophy until Scott joined him on the Ducks. They won a title together in 2007.

Rob (left) and Scott Niedermayer

ARIZONA COYOTES

First Season: 1979–1980

Franchise Record: 1,121–1,206–266–105
Home Rink: Jobing.com Arena (17,653 capacity) in Glendale, Arizona

STANLEY CUPS
None

In 1979 the four remaining World Hockey Association (WHA) teams merged into the NHL. One of those was the Winnipeg Jets, a three-time WHA champion led by former NHL superstar Bobby Hull. The Jets were the WHA's last title winner. The team played 17 seasons in Manitoba, Canada, before leaving in 1996 for the American desert and becoming the Phoenix, and later Arizona, Coyotes.

Coyotes right wing Shane Doan was selected to two All-Star Games.

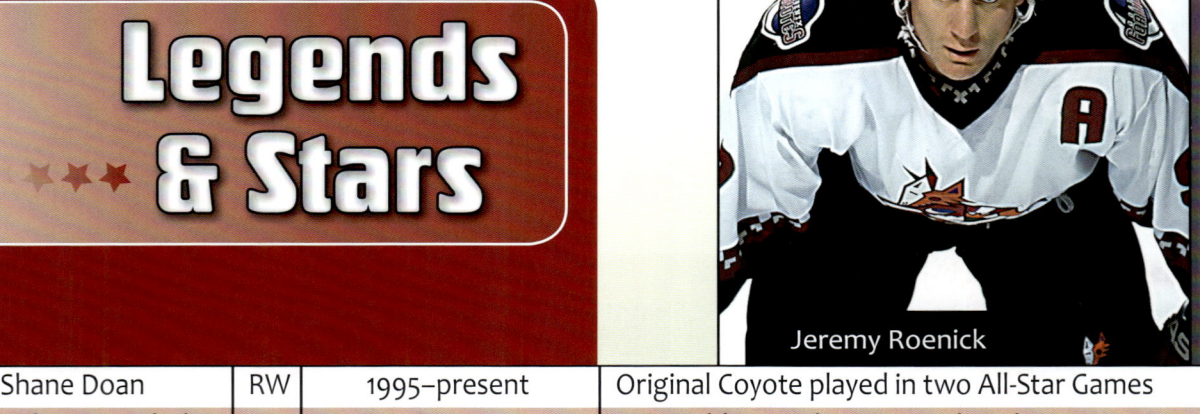
Jeremy Roenick

Shane Doan	RW	1995–present	Original Coyote played in two All-Star Games
Dale Hawerchuk	C	1981–1990	1982 Calder Trophy winner played nine seasons with the Jets
Teppo Numminen	D	1988–2003	Three-time All-Star selection played 15 seasons with the Jets/Coyotes
Jeremy Roenick	C	1996–2001, 2006–2007	Nine-time All-Star Game selection
Keith Tkachuk	LW	1991–2001	Five-time All-Star pick played in Winnipeg and Phoenix

By the Numbers

TOP GOAL SCORER
Dale Hawerchuk
1981–1990
379 goals

TOP GOALTENDER
Ilya Bryzgalov
2007–2011
130 wins

TOP ASSISTS MAN
Thomas Steen
1981–1995
553 assists

TOP DEFENSEMAN
Teppo Numminen
1988–2003
534 points

Zero Tolerance

In 2004 Coyotes goaltender Brian Boucher broke what many thought would be an untouchable record. He set the modern record for consecutive shutouts, blanking teams in five straight games. He kept the puck out of his goal for 332 minutes, 1 second.

Gretzky Joins the Team

Wayne Gretzky played for the Oilers, Kings, Blues, and Rangers. He took on a different role with the Coyotes, becoming a partial owner in 2000. He was also put in charge of managing the hockey team. In 2005 he named himself the team's head coach. Gretzky coached for four seasons, winning 143 games.

BOSTON BRUINS

First Season: 1924–1925

Franchise Record: 2,938–2,240–791–121
Home Rink: TD Garden (17,565 capacity) in Boston, Massachusetts

STANLEY CUPS
1929, 1939, 1941, 1970, 1972, 2011

The Boston Bruins were the first American team to join the Canadian-born NHL. Over their nearly 90 seasons, the Bs have captured six Stanley Cups. One of the best players to ever lace up the skates was a Boston Bruin: the game-changing defenseman Bobby Orr (see page 30).

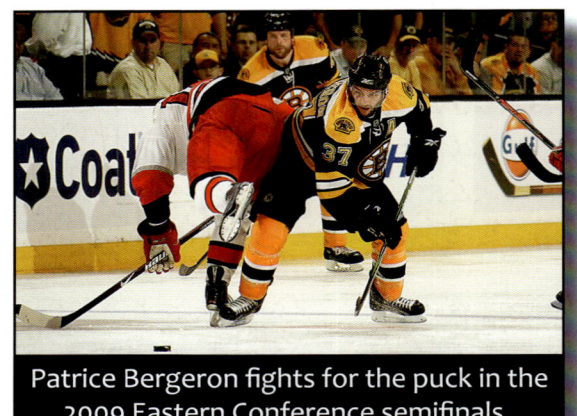
Patrice Bergeron fights for the puck in the 2009 Eastern Conference semifinals.

Legends & Stars

Zdeno Chara

Name	Pos	Years	Notes
Ray Bourque	D	1979–2000	Bruins all-time points leader with 1,506
Frank Brimsek	G	1938–1943, 1945–1949	"Mr. Zero" had 10 shutouts as a rookie; won two Cups
John Bucyk	LW	1957–1978	Played 21 seasons for the Bruins
Zdeno Chara	D	2006–present	Norris Trophy winner is the tallest player in the NHL
Phil Esposito	C	1967–1975	Led the league in scoring five times
Cam Neely	RW	1986–1996	Named to five All-Star Games
Bobby Orr	D	1966–1976	Won eight Norris, three Hart, and two Conn Smythe trophies
Art Ross		1924–1928, 1929–1934, 1936–1939, 1941–1945	Coached 16 seasons, winning 361 games and the 1939 Stanley Cup
Eddie Shore	D	1926–1939	Four-time Hart Trophy winner
Tim Thomas	G	2002–2012	Won the Vezina and Jennings trophies in 2009

By the Numbers

TOP GOAL SCORER
John Bucyk
1957–1978
545 goals

TOP GOALTENDER
Tiny Thompson
1928–1938
252 wins

TOP ASSISTS MAN
Ray Bourque
1979–2000
1,111 assists

TOP DEFENSEMAN
Ray Bourque
1,506 points

Daring Defensemen

Defensemen don't always get the glory—unless they're playing for Boston. The Bruins have had some of the best defensemen to ever play the game. Bobby Orr is considered the best of all time. Eddie Shore was a star in the sport's early days and won four MVPs. Ray Bourque is the top-scoring defenseman of all time.

Bobby Orr (4) in the 1974 NHL playoffs

Breaking Down Barriers

On January 18, 1958, history was made when Bruins winger Willie O'Ree took the ice. O'Ree was the first black player to participate in an NHL game. The Fredericton, New Brunswick, Canada, native had a short professional career. He played in just two games that season and 43 games in 1960–1961. He scored four goals in 1958.

GREAT TEAMS IN FOCUS

1969-1970 BOSTON BRUINS

Bobby Orr was one of the most talented players in hockey history. His greatest moment was scoring the game-winning goal for the 1970 Stanley Cup, and the 1969–1970 Boston Bruins were the best team he played on.

Bobby Orr and Phil Esposito receive awards for their achievements in the 1969–1970 season.

HISTORY BOX

GROWING THE GAME

The Bruins rose to the top of the NHL at an exciting time for the league. For 24 years, the league had consisted of six teams that had been around since 1926 (see page 4). But for the 1967–1968 season, the NHL expanded to Philadelphia, Los Angeles, St. Louis, Minnesota, Pittsburgh, and Oakland. Other professional sports had added teams before. For hockey, this addition was the first step in becoming a major sport. By 2000 the league had grown from 6 to 30 teams.

Great Teams in Focus

1969–1970 Record

Won	Lost	Tied	Playoffs
40	17	19	Defeated New York Rangers 4–2
			Defeated Chicago Blackhawks 4–0
			Defeated St. Louis Blues 4–0

The Bruins won the Cup in 1970 partly thanks to Orr, and partly thanks to a high-scoring center named Phil Esposito. The Bruins had traded for Esposito in 1967. Esposito, then 25 years old, scored 21 goals and 40 assists to finish seventh in the NHL that season. The following season, in 1968–1969, Esposito continued his great offensive play. He became the first player in the league to score more than 100 points. Once he got to Boston, Esposito finished either first or second in scoring in each of the next eight seasons. Behind Esposito and Orr, the Bruins were an unstoppable team.

On the defensive end, the Bruins were very tough. The goalie, Gerry Cheevers, was a colorful character. He painted stitches on his goalie mask to show where pucks had hit him. Orr's defensive play was also changing the game of hockey. Before Orr, defensemen didn't try to score. But Orr liked to skate with the puck and pass. He set up goals like no one else before him. Orr showed that defensemen could do more than just defend. He was the first, and only, defenseman to win a scoring title, with 120 points in 1969–1970. That year, Orr also set an NHL record for 87 assists. He could score, pass, and defend, and this made him one of the game's great players.

During the regular season, the Bruins played in the Eastern Division, which was a very close division. Only seven points separated the first- through fifth-place teams. Meanwhile, the Western Division was very different. The St. Louis Blues won, winning their division by 18 points.

The Blues and the Bruins met in the Stanley Cup finals. In the first game, the Bruins came out strong, scoring an amazing four goals in the third period for an easy 6–1 victory over St. Louis. John Bucyk led Boston, and he scored a hat trick (three goals) for his team, with a goal coming in each period. In Game 2, Boston once again showed they were the better team by scoring six goals. They won the game 6–2.

GREAT TEAMS IN FOCUS

In Game 3, St. Louis showed they weren't going to back down as they took an early lead. The Bruins fought back behind goals from Bucyk and John McKenzie, and the team took a small 2–1 lead in the third period. In the last period, it was Boston's game, as Wayne Cashman scored two goals to give the Bruins a 4–1 victory and a 3–0 series lead. They were now only one game away from a sweep and winning the Stanley Cup.

Bobby Orr (1948-)

Bobby Orr's jersey number—No. 4—is retired in Boston, and he is also honored everywhere that hockey is played. With his skating and skills, he created a new role for defensemen. For Orr, scoring goals was as important as stopping the other team from scoring them. He won three straight Hart trophies as the league's MVP and eight straight Norris trophies as its best defenseman. A bad knee forced him to retire in 1978, after only eight seasons. Orr remains one of the game's greatest players of all time.

Bobby Orr

1969-1970 Boston Bruins

Bobby Orr is tripped after he scores the winning goal against the St. Louis Blues.

St. Louis played very tough in Game 4, with a rough defense and hard-hitting body checks to the Bruins players. It was Boston, however, that scored first. St. Louis came back and scored two quick goals to take a 2–1 lead. Boston's regular season star, Esposito, tied the game at 2–2. The Blues' Larry Keenan scored early in the last period to give the Blues a slim 3–2 lead. With six minutes left, Boston scored again, tying the game at 3–3. The game was forced into overtime.

Orr's greatest moment came in overtime. He flipped the puck into the goal for the game winner. Right after he scored, Orr was tripped up by Noel Picard. He went flying arms first through the air, completely level with the ice. The photo of that moment is one of the most famous hockey images of all time. The Stanley Cup victory was one of the great moments in the history of the city of Boston, which had waited 29 years to win the Cup again. Fans would have to wait only two years for the next, with Orr again scoring the series-winning goals.

BUFFALO SABRES

First Season: 1970–1971

Franchise Record: 1,611–1,291–409–99

Home Rink: First Niagara Center (18,690 capacity) in Buffalo, New York

STANLEY CUPS
None

When the NHL expanded for the first time after doubling the league in 1967, it added a team in Buffalo, New York. Buffalo had a successful minor-league hockey team for 30 years. The Sabres continued that success, reaching two Stanley Cup finals. However, they fell short of a championship each time, despite stars Gilbert Perreault and Dominik Hasek leading the way.

Sabres right wing Mike Grier (25)

Legends & Stars

Dominik Hasek (39)

Name	Pos	Years	Notes
Dominik Hasek	G	1992–2001	Won both of his Hart trophies and six Vezina trophies while playing for Buffalo
Pat LaFontaine	C	1991–1997	Retired as the second-highest-scoring American-born player with 1,013 points
Rick Martin	LW	1971–1981	Selected to seven All-Star Games
Ryan Miller	G	2002–2014	Selected to U.S. Olympic team in 2010
Gilbert Perreault	C	1970–1987	High-scoring forward won the Calder Trophy in 1971

By the Numbers

TOP GOAL SCORER
Gilbert Perreault
1970–1987
512 goals

TOP GOALTENDER
Ryan Miller
2002–2014
269 wins

TOP ASSISTS MAN
Gilbert Perreault
814 assists

TOP DEFENSEMAN
Phil Housley
1982–1990
558 points

The French Connection

In the Sabres' early years, the trio of Gilbert Perreault, René Robert, and Rick Martin was a dominating forward line. Since they were all from French-speaking Quebec, the group was dubbed The French Connection. Their nickname was also the name of a popular movie at the time. The line led the Sabres to the 1975 finals, where they lost to the Philadelphia Flyers.

NHL Winter Classic

Outdoor Hockey

The first NHL Winter Classic, an annual New Year's Day outdoor game, took place in Buffalo's Ralph Wilson Stadium in 2008. The Sabres lost to the Pittsburgh Penguins in a shootout that snowy day. It was just the second regular-season outdoor game in NHL history.

CALGARY FLAMES

Franchise Record: 1,491–1,279–379–105
Home Rink: Scotiabank Saddledome (19,289 capacity) in Calgary, Alberta, Canada

STANLEY CUP
1989

First Season: 1972–1973

When the NHL expanded by two teams in 1972, the Canadian province of Alberta wasn't even considered. Instead, Atlanta was the choice, and the Flames were born. But after eight years and limited success, the team packed up and headed north to hockey country. In Calgary the Flames have played for three Stanley Cups, winning the prized trophy once.

David Moss

Legends & Stars

Miikka Kiprusoff

Theoren Fleury	RW	1988–1998	Seven-time All-Star Game participant
Jarome Iginla	RW	1996–2013	Six-time All-Star led the NHL in scoring twice
Miikka Kiprusoff	G	2003–2013	Awarded the Vezina Trophy in 2006
Al MacInnis	D	1981–1994	Won the Conn Smythe Trophy in 1989

By the Numbers

TOP GOAL SCORER
Jarome Iginla
1996–2013
525 goals

TOP GOALTENDER
Miikka Kiprusoff
2003–2013
305 wins

TOP ASSISTS MAN
Al MacInnis
1981–1994
609 assists

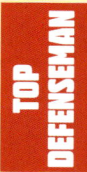
TOP DEFENSEMAN
Al MacInnis
822 points

Rare Win

The Flames captured the 1989 Stanley Cup by winning Game 6 of the finals. That game took place in Montreal, home of the mighty Canadiens. The win was significant because Flames veteran Lanny McDonald and his teammates became the first visiting team to celebrate a championship in the Canadiens' rink.

Calgary coach Darryl Sutter led the Flames to two playoff appearances.

All in the Family

The Sutter boys from tiny Viking, Alberta, are a hockey success story. Six brothers—Brent, Brian, Darryl, Duane, Rich, and Ron—all made it to the NHL. The Sutters have a close connection with the Flames. Ron played for the team, and Brent, Brian, and Darryl all coached it. Darryl led Calgary to the Cup finals in 2004. Two of the brothers' sons also played in the NHL. Darryl's son Brett debuted with the Flames in 2008–2009.

CAROLINA HURRICANES

First Season: 1979–1980

Franchise Record: 1,104–1,230–263–101

Home Rink: PNC Arena (18,730 capacity) in Raleigh, North Carolina

STANLEY CUP
2006

The Carolina Hurricanes' history goes back to another city and another league. They started as the New England Whalers of the World Hockey Association (WHA) in 1972 and were one of four WHA teams to merge into the NHL in 1979 (see page 24). After spending 18 more seasons in Hartford, Connecticut, the team moved to Raleigh, North Carolina, in 1997 and became the Hurricanes.

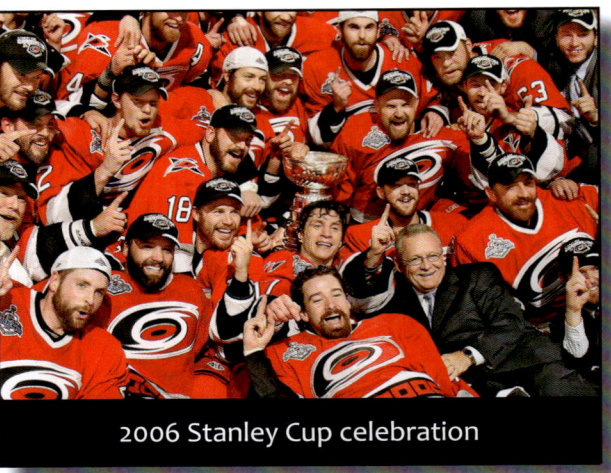
2006 Stanley Cup celebration

Legends & Stars

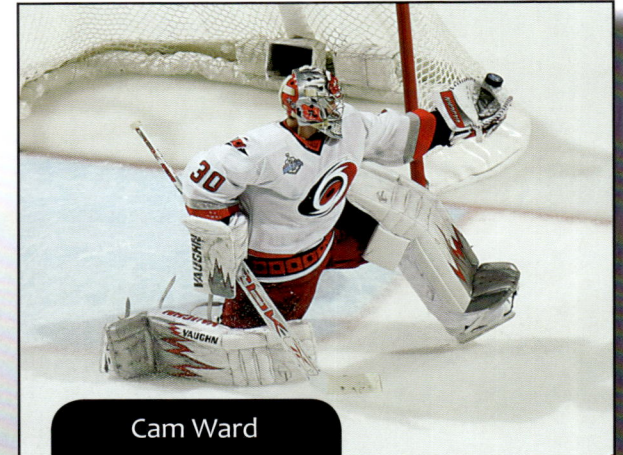
Cam Ward

Rod Brind'Amour	C	2000–2010	Twice named the NHL's top defensive forward
Ron Francis	C	1981–1991, 1998–2004	Ranks second all-time in assists, third all-time in games played
Eric Staal	C	2003–present	Four-time All-Star Game pick
Cam Ward	G	2005–present	Won the Conn Smythe Trophy in 2006

By the Numbers

TOP GOAL SCORER 	**Ron Francis** 1981–1991, 1998–2004 382 goals	**TOP GOALTENDER** 	**Cam Ward** 2005–present 224 wins
TOP ASSISTS MAN 	**Ron Francis** 793 assists	**TOP DEFENSEMAN**	**Dave Babych** 1986–1991 240 points

And Howe (and Howe and Howe)

In 1977 the Whalers lured hockey legend Gordie Howe and his sons, defensemen Mark and Marty, to play for the team. They skated together for three seasons, including one year in the NHL when Gordie Howe was 51 years old. The longtime Red Wings star scored 15 goals and had 26 assists in his 32nd and final full year of professional hockey.

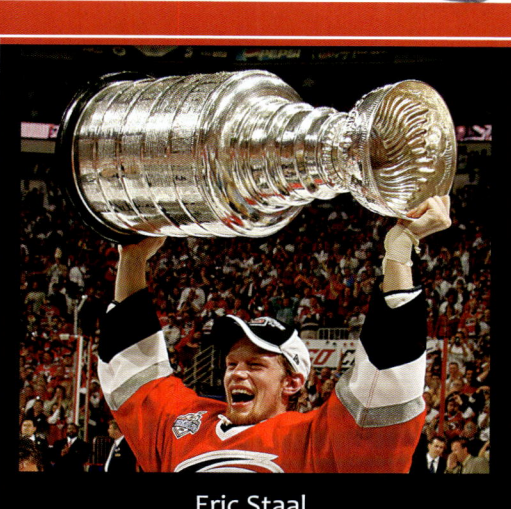

Eric Staal

Carolina Cup

The Hurricanes made it to the Stanley Cup finals in 2002, but they fell to the mighty Red Wings. Four years later, though, high-scoring center Eric Staal was skating the famous trophy around the rink after defeating the Edmonton Oilers. It was the state of North Carolina's first professional sports championship.

CHICAGO BLACKHAWKS

First Season: 1926–1927

Franchise Record: 2,542–2,556–814–112
Home Rink: United Center (19,717 capacity) in Chicago, Illinois

STANLEY CUPS
1934, 1938, 1961, 2010, 2013

One of the NHL's "Original Six" teams, the Chicago Blackhawks were founded by coffee tycoon Major Frederic McLaughlin. To fill up his first roster, McLaughlin purchased Oregon's Portland Rosebuds of the Western Hockey League. Then he moved most of the players to the Windy City.

Commissioner Gary Bettman hands the 2013 Stanley Cup to Jonathan Toews (19).

Legends & Stars

Patrick Kane

Name	Pos	Years	Notes
Chris Chelios	D	1990–1999	Won two of his three Norris trophies as a Blackhawk
Tony Esposito	G	1969–1984	Three-time Vezina Trophy winner and six-time All-Star
Glenn Hall	G	1957–1967	Three-time Vezina Trophy winner appeared in 502 consecutive games
Bobby Hull	LW	1957–1972	Won two Hart trophies and played in 12 All-Star Games
Patrick Kane	RW	2007–present	Won the Calder Trophy in 2008
Stan Mikita	C/RW	1958–1980	Two-time Hart and Lady Byng trophy winner
Pierre Pilote	D	1955–1968	Won the Norris Trophy three times in a row
Denis Savard	C	1980–1990, 1995–1997	Seven-time All-Star Game selection
Jonathan Toews	C	2007–present	All-Rookie pick was named captain in his second season

By the Numbers

TOP GOAL SCORER
Bobby Hull
1957–1972
604 goals

TOP GOALTENDER
Tony Esposito
1969–1984
418 wins

TOP ASSISTS MAN
Stan Mikita
1958–1980
926 assists

TOP DEFENSEMAN
Doug Wilson
1977–1991
779 points

Unlikely Championship

In 1938 the Blackhawks went 14–25–9 but managed to slip into the playoffs. Led by American goaltender Mike Karakas, Chicago upset the Montreal Canadiens and the New York Americans. Then they defeated the Toronto Maple Leafs in the Stanley Cup finals three games to one for their second championship.

Bobby Hull

The Golden Jet

In the late 1950s, a speedy, blond-haired left wing burst onto the ice for the Blackhawks. Bobby Hull, nicknamed "The Golden Jet" because of his yellow locks, could fire a slap shot up to 120 miles (193 kilometers) per hour. To make matters worse for goaltenders, he was one of the first players to add a curve to the blade of his stick, which made the puck fly unpredictably.

COLORADO AVALANCHE

Franchise Record: 1,242–1,108–261–87
Home Rink: Pepsi Center (18,007 capacity) in Denver, Colorado

STANLEY CUPS
1996, 2001

First Season: 1979–1980

The NHL didn't last long its first time in Denver. In 1982 after just six years, the Colorado Rockies became the New Jersey Devils. But in 1995 another struggling franchise was on the move. The Quebec Nordiques, a World Hockey Association team that had merged into the NHL, moved west and became the Colorado Avalanche.

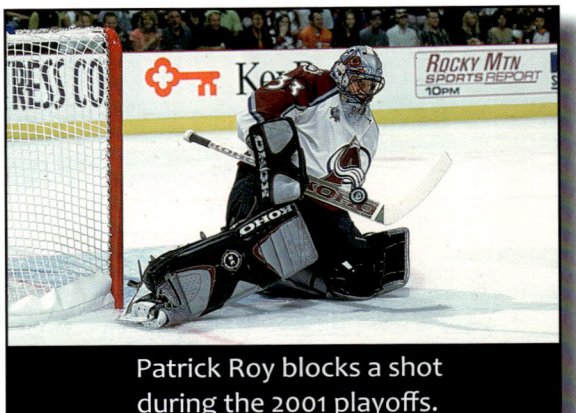
Patrick Roy blocks a shot during the 2001 playoffs.

Peter Forsberg

Peter Forsberg	C	1994–2004, 2007–2008	Owns a Calder and a Hart trophy
Milan Hejduk	RW	1998–present	Led the NHL in goals in 2002–2003
Patrick Roy	G	1995–2003	Three-time Vezina Trophy winner ranks No. 2 on all-time wins list
Joe Sakic	C	1988–2009	1996 Conn Smythe winner and 2001 Hart Trophy winner
Paul Stastny	C	2006–2014	Named to U.S. Olympic Team in 2010
Peter Stastny	C	1980–1990	Was the Nordiques' all-time leading scorer; still ranks second on the franchise list

By the Numbers

TOP GOAL SCORER	Joe Sakic 1988–2009 625 goals	**TOP GOALTENDER**	Patrick Roy 1995–2003 262 wins
TOP ASSISTS MAN	Joe Sakic 1,016 assists	**TOP DEFENSEMAN**	Adam Foote 1991–2004, 2008–2011 259 points

Stastny Scores

In the early 1980s, three brothers from the country formerly known as Czechoslovakia—Peter, Anton, and Marian Stastny—went to Canada and played for the Quebec Nordiques. Peter became one of the top scorers not named Gretzky to skate in the NHL. The Nordiques retired Stastny's No. 26 jersey, but his son, Paul wore it for the Avs for eight seasons when he was with the team.

Paul Stastny

Ready to Win

In their last season in Quebec City, the Nordiques lost in the first round of the post-season. But with players such as Joe Sakic, Peter Forsberg, Valeri Kamensky, and Claude Lemieux, the franchise was ready for greatness. The next season the team had transformed into the Avalanche, traded for Hall-of-Fame goaltender Patrick Roy, and won the Stanley Cup.

GREAT TEAMS IN FOCUS

2000-2001 COLORADO AVALANCHE

After moving to Denver from Quebec City in 1995, the Avalanche quickly became one of the NHL's most successful franchises. Joe Sakic and Peter Forsberg, two of the game's best forwards, were already on board as well as the game's best goalie, Patrick Roy. They won their first Stanley Cup in 1996.

The Avalanche score against the New Jersey Devils in Game 1 of the Stanley Cup finals.

For the team's 2000–2001 season, they were joined by a new star. Ray Bourque was one of the best defensemen of his generation. He had spent all 20 seasons of his career in Boston. After two unsuccessful trips to the finals with the Bruins, Bourque wanted another chance to win the Cup before his career ended. He asked for a trade to Colorado in 2000.

That year, the Avalanche had the best regular season record, 52–16–10–4 (Wins–Losses–Ties–Overtime Losses). Roy made history as he broke Terry Sawchuck's record for career wins, with 448. After avoiding Detroit and Dallas in the playoffs, the Avalanche would face the Devils in the finals. Bourque and Colorado could not be stopped.

Great Teams in Focus

2000-2001 Record

Won	Lost	Tied	OTL	Playoffs
52	16	10	4	Defeated Vancouver Canucks 4–0
				Defeated Los Angeles Kings 4–3
				Defeated St. Louis Blues 4–1
				Defeated New Jersey Devils 4–3

Bourque's motto was "16W"—the number of wins needed to win the Cup, and the exit off the New Jersey Turnpike that led to the Meadowlands, where the Devils played.

In Game 1, the Avalanche came out strong behind two goals from star Sakic and one each from Rob Blake, Chris Drury, and Steven Reinprecht. The Avalanche won easily, 5–0, shutting out the Devils. Roy was great in the win, stopping all 26 shots he faced. It was his third playoff shutout, and eighteenth of the year, as he extended his Stanley Cup winning streak to nine games.

New Jersey came back in Game 2. Colorado's Sakic scored the first goal of the game with only six minutes played, but his team would not score again. The Devils came back in the first period. Neither of the teams scored again, but that was enough to lead New Jersey to a 2–1 victory, as they tied the series up at 1–1.

The Avalanche started out Game 3 losing 1–0, but Martin Skoula, Bourque, and Dan Hinote all scored goals, giving their team a 3–1 victory and a 2–1 series lead. However, New Jersey wasn't about to lose two games in a row. They outshot the Avalanche 35–12 in Game 4 and ended up with a 3–2 victory. The series was tied 2–2.

HISTORY BOX

THE DEAD PUCK ERA

The Colorado Avalanche were one of the few teams in the league with plenty of offensive talent. At this time, most teams were concentrating on defense and making it almost impossible for other teams to score. When the Devils won the Cup in 1995, they did it with a system known as the "neutral-zone trap," which puts lots of players in the middle of the ice and reduces offensive chances. By 2000 nearly every team in the league was using a method of the trap. In 1983–1984 the Oilers scored 446 goals. In 2002–2003 no team scored more than 269, and two teams scored fewer than two goals per game.

GREAT TEAMS IN FOCUS

Patrick Roy

Patrick Roy retired in 2003 with a claim to the title of hockey's greatest goaltender ever. He won the Stanley Cup with Montreal as a rookie in 1986, and he then led the Canadiens to glory in 1993. But in December 1995, Montreal coach Mario Tremblay refused to take him out of the net on a night when the Canadiens lost 11–1. When he was finally replaced, Roy said he would never play for Montreal again. Traded to Colorado, he led the Avalanche to the Stanley Cup that season and another in 2001. He is the NHL's all-time leader in games played by a goalie (1,029), wins (551), and playoff wins (151).

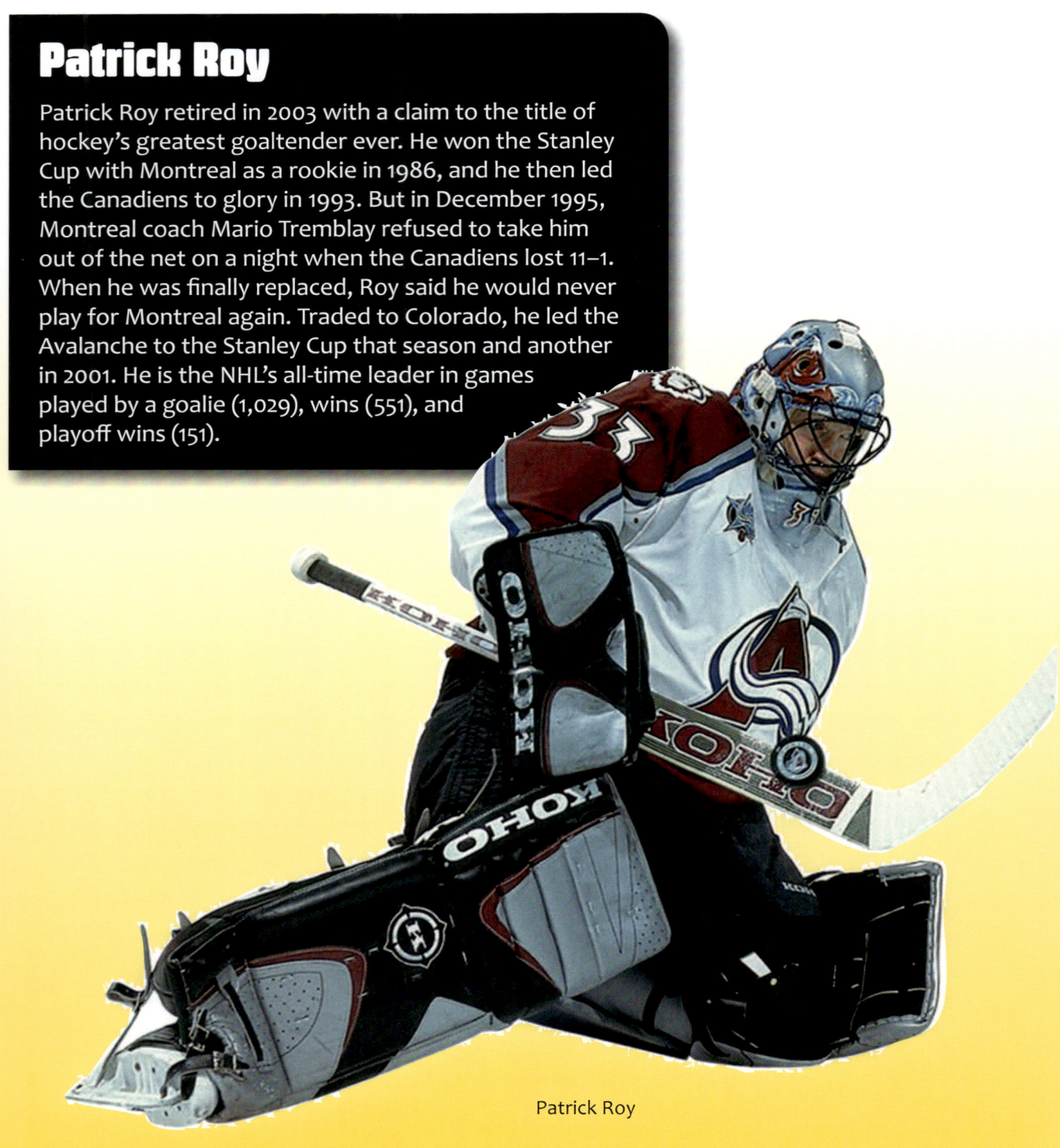

Patrick Roy

2000-2001 Colorado Avalanche

Game 5 went to New Jersey, who won 4–1. This loss was Colorado's worst loss of the post-season. Until this game, they had not trailed in the playoffs by more than one goal. It was also the first time they lost back-to-back playoff games. Instead of feeling sorry for themselves, they came out strong in Game 6. Roy recorded his second shutout of the series, and fourth of the playoffs, as Colorado won 4–0. Roy blocked all 24 shots that came at him, including 12 in the first period. Adam Foote, Ville Nieminen, Drury, and Alex Tanguay all scored goals for the Avalanche, tying the series at 3–3. This forced a seventh game at their home arena.

No one in the history of the NHL waited as long as Bourque to win the Stanley Cup, and he finally got it in Game 7. Sakic scored a goal and assisted on one in the game, bringing his total to 13 goals and 13 assists for the playoffs. Tanguay was the star of the game, scoring two goals to lead the Avalanche to a 3–1 victory, and their second Stanley Cup in five years. Roy had 25 stops, and because of his excellent play in the playoffs, he was awarded the Conn Smythe Trophy.

After the victory, NHL Commissioner Gary Bettman handed the Cup to Avalanche captain Sakic to hoist above his head. But instead of lifting the Cup, Sakic passed it to Bourque. After 22 seasons in the NHL, Bourque capped his Hall of Fame career by raising the Cup above his head.

A promising team became a great one after Ray Bourque joined.

COLUMBUS BLUE JACKETS

First Season: 2000–2001

Franchise Record: 409–490–33–100
Home Rink: Nationwide Arena (18,136 capacity) in Columbus, Ohio

STANLEY CUPS
NONE

The second go-round of NHL hockey in Ohio has been more successful than the first. In 1976 the California Golden Seals moved to Cleveland and became known as the Barons. But that team lasted just two seasons before folding. More than 20 years later, Ohio's capital, Columbus, was awarded an expansion team, and the Blue Jackets were born.

Raffi Torres (14) controls the puck near the Red Wings' net during the 2009 playoffs.

Legends & Stars

Steve Mason (1)

Sergei Bobrovsky	G	2012–present	Won the Vezina Trophy in 2013
Rostislav Klesla	D	2000–2011	Selected to the NHL All-Rookie Team in 2001–2002
Steve Mason	G	2008–2013	Calder Trophy winner and Vezina runner-up in 2009
Rick Nash	LW	2002–2012	Five-time All-Star led the league in goals in 2004
R. J. Umberger	C	2008-present	Ranks third in franchise history in points

By the Numbers

TOP GOAL SCORER 	**Rick Nash** 2002–2012 289 goals	**TOP GOALTENDER** 	**Steve Mason** 2008–2013 96 wins
TOP ASSISTS MAN	**Rick Nash** 258 assists	**TOP DEFENSEMAN**	**Fedor Tyutin** 2008–present 141 points

Young Gun

Columbus made the right call picking Rick Nash with the No. 1 overall draft pick in 2002. By the end of the 2003–2004 season, the 19-year-old Nash was the youngest player in NHL history to lead the league in goals. He was also an All-Star that season, becoming the youngest to play in the game since 1986.

Rick Nash (61) won the Maurice Richard Trophy in 2003–2004.

Tragedy at the Rink

In 2002 Brittanie Cecil, a 13-year-old fan, was struck by a puck that had deflected into the stands at Nationwide Arena. She died two days later from the injury. She was the first fan to die in the 85-year history of the NHL. As a result the teams decided to hang netting behind the goals at all arenas to prevent such a tragedy from happening again.

DALLAS STARS

First Season: 1967–1968

Franchise Record: 1,572-1,510-459-95
Home Rink: American Airlines Center (18,000 capacity) in Dallas, Texas

STANLEY CUP
1999

Brett Hull (22) takes a shot against the Colorado Avalanche during the 1999 playoffs.

For 26 seasons the North Stars played in the Twin Cities of Minneapolis and St. Paul. But in 1993 the team moved to Texas, dropped the word North from its name, and became the Dallas Stars. In Minnesota the Stars went to two Stanley Cup finals, but they finally won a title in Dallas in 1999.

Legends & Stars

Marty Turco (35)

Ed Belfour	G	1997–2002	Allowed the fewest goals in the NHL four times
Neal Broten	C	1980–1995, 1996–1997	Team's all-time leading scorer during the Minnesota years
Loui Eriksson	LW	2006–2013	Left wing became an All-Star in 2011
Mike Modano	C	1989–2010	Named to seven All-Star Games in 20 years with the Stars
Joe Nieuwendyk	C	1995–2002	Conn Smythe Trophy winner in 1999
Marty Turco	G	2000–2010	Three-time All-Star Game selection

By the Numbers

TOP GOAL SCORER — Mike Modano, 1989–2010, 557 goals

TOP GOALTENDER — Marty Turco, 2000–2010, 262 wins

TOP ASSISTS MAN — Mike Modano, 802 assists

TOP DEFENSEMAN — Sergei Zubov, 1996–2009, 549 points

Epic Win

When Brett Hull scored the Stanley Cup-clinching goal in the third overtime of Game 6 in the 1999 finals, it was the end of a marathon night. The Stars and the Sabres battled for 114 minutes, 51 seconds and combined for 104 shots on goal. Dallas goalie Ed Belfour made 53 saves in the 2-1 Stars victory.

Stars right wing Pat Verbeek (16) fights for the puck during the 1999 Stanley Cup finals.

American Hero

The Minnesota North Stars drafted Mike Modano with the No. 1 overall pick in 1988. He played 20 of his 21 seasons with the Stars. As well as being the franchise's all-time leading scorer, he was also the NHL's top scoring American-born player. He finished his career with 1,374 points.

DETROIT RED WINGS

First Season: 1926–1927

Franchise Record: 2,774–2,328–815–107
Home Rink: Joe Louis Arena (20,066 capacity) in Detroit, Michigan

STANLEY CUPS
1936, 1937, 1943, 1950, 1952, 1954, 1955, 1997, 1998, 2002, 2008

With 11 NHL championships—more than any other hockey team in the United States—Detroit earned the nickname "Hockeytown." Only the Canadiens and the Maple Leafs have more Stanley Cup wins. First known as the Detroit Cougars and then the Falcons, the team became the Red Wings in 1932.

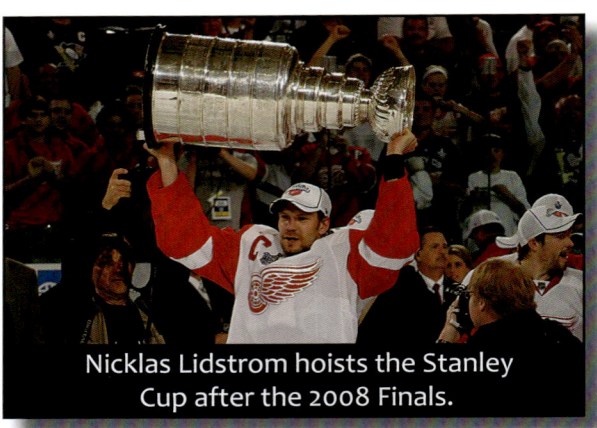
Nicklas Lidstrom hoists the Stanley Cup after the 2008 Finals.

Legends & Stars

Terry Sawchuk

Jack Adams		1927–1947	Wings' second coach won three championships in 20 years
Alex Delvecchio	C/LW	1950–1974	Named to the All-Star Game 13 times in 24 seasons
Sergei Fedorov	C	1990–2003	Won the Hart Trophy once and the Frank J. Selke Trophy twice
Gordie Howe	RW	1946–1971	Six-time Hart Trophy winner ranks third on the all-time points list
Red Kelly	D	1947–1960	Captured four Lady Byng awards and one Norris Trophy
Nicklas Lidstrom	D	1991–2012	Owns seven Norris trophies and one Conn Smythe Trophy
Ted Lindsay	LW	1944–1957, 1964–1965	Captained three Stanley Cup winners in the 1950s
Chris Osgood	G	1993–2001, 2005–2011	Two-time Jennings Trophy winner
Terry Sawchuk	G	1949–1955, 1957–1964, 1968–1969	Four-time Vezina Trophy winner
Steve Yzerman	C	1983–2006	1998 Conn Smythe winner played 22 seasons in Detroit

By the Numbers

TOP GOAL SCORER
Gordie Howe
1946–1971
786 goals

TOP ASSISTS MAN
Steve Yzerman
1983–2006
1,063 assists

TOP GOALTENDER
Terry Sawchuk
1949–1955, 1957–1964, 1968–1969
351 wins

TOP DEFENSEMAN
Nicklas Lidstrom
1991–2012
1,142 points

Mr. Hockey

There's a reason Gordie Howe got the nickname "Mr. Hockey": He could do it all. In more than 25 seasons in Detroit, Howe led the league in scoring six times. In 14 other seasons, he ranked among the top five, and he finished his NHL career with 1,850 points and four championships. (For more on Howe, turn to page 52.)

Throwing the Octopus

A slimy tradition started in 1952. That's when a dead octopus was first thrown onto the ice during a Red Wings home playoff game for good luck. The creature's eight legs then represented the eight wins a team needed to win the Stanley Cup. Even though more games are now needed, the smelly tradition continues.

GREAT TEAMS IN FOCUS

1954-1955 DETROIT RED WINGS

Detroit Red Wings star Gordie Howe played hockey throughout five decades and enjoyed individual success throughout his years as a player. Howe won four Stanley Cups with the Red Wings in the early 1950s. The Detroit Red Wings finished first in the league seven straight times from 1948–1949 through 1954–1955.

Gordie Howe (1928-)

Gordie Howe was among the NHL's top-five scorers for 20 straight seasons. He led the league in scoring six times and was named MVP six times. In the process Howe set records for games played, points, goals, and assists.

It wasn't until Wayne Gretzky came along that Howe's records were broken. The two played together in the World Hockey Association (WHA). In 1979–1980, when that league merged with the NHL, Gretzky's first NHL season was Howe's last. In 1997 Howe actually played with the minor-league Detroit Vipers to reach the milestone of five decades of playing pro hockey.

Great Teams in Focus

In addition to Howe, the Red Wings were a great team. In 1954–1955, the Red Wings had the best offensive attack in hockey, with the high-scoring, hard-hitting "Production Line" of Howe, "Terrible" Ted Lindsay, and Alex Delvecchio. In 1952–1953, Howe led the league with 95 points, and Lindsay was second with 71, as the Red Wings scored 222 goals. None of the other five teams in the NHL scored more than 169 goals.

Terry Sawchuk

HISTORY BOX
THE MOTOR CITY WORK ETHIC

"The Production Line" was a good nickname for the Red Wings' top forward line of Gordie Howe, Ted Lindsay, and Alex Delvecchio. Not only could that line score lots of goals, the players also represented the spirit of the city. In the years after World War II (1939–1945), there was a huge growth of the auto industry in Detroit, Michigan. Many fans worked on the production line in an auto plant, such as Ford's massive River Rouge complex, and then relaxed by watching the Red Wings play. In a hardworking city, the Red Wings were especially appreciated because they tried hard in every game.

After their seventh straight first-place finish, the Red Wings faced the Toronto Maple Leafs in the first round of the playoffs. They easily beat Toronto in four games, moving on to the Stanley Cup finals, where they faced the Montreal Canadiens. The Canadiens had reached the finals for their fifth straight year. The two teams had met earlier in the regular season, when both teams were tied for first place. Montreal's fans had gotten out of control and started a riot.

GREAT TEAMS IN FOCUS

Inside the arena, the fans threw food, programs, and a tear gas bomb. Outside, they ran wild in the street, smashing windows and breaking into stores and cars. Because of the riot, tensions between the teams and their fans were very high. It would be an interesting matchup.

In Game 1 of the Stanley Cup finals, Detroit's Marty Pavelich and Lindsay scored goals late in the game to lead the Red Wings to a 4–2 victory. Lindsay continued his great playing in Game 2, scoring an amazing four goals to lead the Red Wings to an easy 7–1 victory. Marcel Pronovost, Howe, and Delvecchio also scored for Detroit. Detroit now led the

Ted Lindsay scored many goals for the Red Wings.

1954-1955 Detroit Red Wings

1954-1955 Record

Won	Lost	Tied	Playoffs
42	17	11	Defeated Toronto Maple Leafs 4–0
			Defeated Montreal Canadiens 4–3

series, 2–0. However, Montreal didn't give up. They came back in Game 3 and won behind Bernie "Boom-Boom" Geoffrion's two goals. Montreal then used the momentum from their Game 3 win and won Game 4 against Detroit, 5–3. Earl "Dutch" Reibel tried to keep the Red Wings in the game by scoring two goals, but it just wasn't enough.

The series was now tied 2–2. Playing great like he had been all season, Howe scored a hat trick for his team, and they cruised to a 5–1 victory in Game 5. All Detroit needed was one more victory to win the Stanley Cup, but Montreal wasn't ready to give up. In Game 6 the Canadiens showed they wanted to be champions just as much as the Red Wings did. They won 6–3. The series was now tied 3–3, and the final Game 7 would determine which team would be crowned champion. People started to call the series a "homer's series," because every victory in the series was won at the home team's arena.

Game 7 was intense. It was at the Red Wings' arena, and the team hadn't lost a home game in four months. The "Production Line" carried them through. They weren't going to let the Canadiens beat them at home, and they won an exciting 3–1 game to clinch the Stanley Cup. Delvecchio was the offensive star of the game, scoring two goals, while Howe added one, his ninth goal of the playoffs. Howe set a playoff record with 20 points in 11 games. The victory gave Detroit's general manager, Jack Adams, his seventh Stanley Cup!

EDMONTON OILERS

First Season: 1979–1980

Franchise Record: 1,224–1,102–262–110
Home Rink: Rexall Place (16,839 capacity) in Edmonton, Alberta, Canada

STANLEY CUPS
1984, 1985, 1987, 1988, 1990

One of four World Hockey Association (WHA) teams to join the NHL, the Edmonton Oilers became a dynasty in the 1980s, thanks to "The Great One"—Wayne Gretzky. The superstar and his high-flying, high-scoring supporting cast scored 400 goals a season five years in a row. That run included an NHL-record 446 goals over 80 games (5.6 per game) during the Alberta team's first Stanley Cup season in 1983–1984. (For more on this amazing season, turn the page.)

Coach Craig MacTavish won more than 300 games in eight seasons with the Oilers.

Legends & Stars

Taylor Hall

Glenn Anderson	RW	1980–1991, 1996	Four-time All-Star Game selection
Paul Coffey	D	1980–1987	Three-time Norris Trophy winner and a 14-time All-Star Game pick
Grant Fuhr	G	1981–1991	Won the Vezina Trophy in 1988
Wayne Gretzky	C	1978–1988	NHL's all-time leading scorer won nine Hart trophies in 10 years
Taylor Hall	LW	2010–present	NHL's top overall pick in 2010
Jari Kurri	RW	1980–1990	Ranks second on the Oilers' all-time scoring list
Mark Messier	C	1979–1991	Two-time MVP ranks second on the NHL's all-time points list
Glen Sather		1976–1989, 1993–1994	Edmonton coach led the Oilers to four Stanley Cup championships

56

By the Numbers

 **TOP GOAL SCORER** — Wayne Gretzky 1978–1988, 583 goals

 **TOP GOALTENDER** — Grant Fuhr 1981–1991, 226 wins

 **TOP ASSISTS MAN** — Wayne Gretzky 1,086 assists

 **TOP DEFENSEMAN** — Paul Coffey 1980–1987, 669 points

How Great?

It's safe to say that Wayne Gretzky's records will never be broken. Number 99 was the only player to score more than 200 points in a season. He accomplished the feat four times, including a record 215-point performance (52 goals, 163 assists) in 1985–1986. Gretzky scored a record 92 goals in 1981–1982. His career-points mark of 2,857 includes 1,963 assists, which is more than the total points compiled by anyone else who's ever played.

Mess and the Rest

If people needed proof that the Oilers were more than just Wayne Gretzky, they got it in 1990. Two years after Gretzky was traded to the Kings (see page 59), Edmonton won another Stanley Cup. That team included captain Mark Messier and six others who were part of all five of the Oilers' championships.

GREAT TEAMS IN FOCUS

1983-1984 EDMONTON OILERS

The greatest player the game of hockey has ever known, Wayne Gretzky, could do anything. He set records for goals, assists, and points in a career and in a single season that may never be broken. He retired with 61 NHL records. He played on many great teams, but the 1983–1984 Edmonton Oilers were the best.

To win his first Stanley Cup, Gretzky had to beat the New York Islanders in 1984. The Islanders had won four Stanley Cups in a row, and in 1982–1983, the Islanders had beaten the Oilers for the Cup. The Oilers' coach, Glen Sather, had promised that the next season his team would score 100 points, win the division, and win the Stanley Cup. Sather stuck to his word, as the 1983–1984 Oilers achieved every goal he set for them. Edmonton won the Cup and became hockey's new dynasty. The Oilers would win four Cups in five years.

With Gretzky in the middle, the Oilers were the best offensive team ever. The 1983–1984 Oilers won 57 games and set a record with 446 goals. Gretzky, Jari Kurri, and Glenn Anderson all scored 50 or more goals for the Oilers. Only the great Mario Lemieux could keep the

Grant Fuhr (1962-)

Grant Fuhr had a tough job. The Oilers scored so many goals that they didn't have to play much defense. That left him alone as the goalie. His statistics weren't very good, so sometimes fans ignored him. But he was also a pioneer, the game's first great black goalie and one of its first black stars. Ten years after Fuhr played in the NHL, there were more than a dozen African American goalies playing at the top level in hockey. Fuhr was inducted into the Hockey Hall of Fame in 2003.

Great Teams in Focus

1983-1984 Record

Won	Lost	Tied	Playoffs
57	18	5	Defeated Winnipeg Jets 3–0
			Defeated Calgary Flames 4–3
			Defeated Minnesota North Stars 4–0
			Defeated New York Islanders 4–1

Oilers from dominating the individual leaders. Twice, the Oilers had three players who were 50-goal scorers and four players who were 100-point scorers. This had never been done before. Grant Fuhr and Mark Messier were also great players.

In the first round of the playoffs, the Oilers faced Winnipeg. The Oilers swept the Jets. In the second round, the Oilers faced a much tougher opponent in the Calgary Flames. The series went all the way to the deciding Game 7, where the Oilers earned the victory to advance to the next round. In the semifinals, the Oilers faced Minnesota, who they easily swept to earn their spot in the Stanley Cup finals.

It was the second straight year they had reached the finals, where they met the New York Islanders, who had beaten them the previous year and were going for their fifth-straight Cup. It would be a great series.

Game 1 of the finals was a great defensive match. No team scored in the first two periods, as Oilers goalie Fuhr and Islanders goalie Billy Smith played incredibly in the net. Someone had to score, and in the third period, Oilers player Kevin McClelland broke free for a goal. It was all Edmonton needed as they shut out the defending champions 1–0.

New York showed why they had won four straight Cups in Game 2 as Clark Gillies scored a hat trick. The Islanders coasted to an easy 6–1 victory, tying the series at 1–1. The teams switched roles in Game 3, as Edmonton did most of the scoring. Edmonton's Glenn Anderson and Paul Coffey scored two goals only 17 seconds apart. They eventually scored five more goals, three coming in the last period, for an easy 7–2 victory. Edmonton now led the series 2–1.

GREAT TEAMS IN FOCUS

Gretzky scored two goals in Game 4 as the Oilers won again, 7–2. Edmonton led the series 3–1 against the defending champions. With a chance for the Oilers to earn the Stanley Cup if they won in Game 5, Gretzky came out playing great. He scored the first two goals of the game, both on assists by Kurri. Gretzky then showed that he could pass, too, as he assisted Ken Linseman for a goal. Kurri scored one himself and gave the Oilers a strong 4–0 lead. The Islanders tried to come back, but Edmonton was just too strong. The Oilers ended up winning 5–2, clinching the Stanley Cup.

On August 9, 1988, the hockey world was shocked when the Oilers traded Gretzky and two other players to the Kings for two players, three first-round picks, and cash. The Oilers had won four Cups with Gretzky. They won one after he left, but the team was never as good as they were in 1984.

Wayne Gretzky lifts the Stanley Cup in 1984.

1983-1984 Edmonton Oilers

HISTORY BOX

GRETZKY GOES WEST

The trade that sent Wayne Gretzky west to the Los Angeles Kings was very surprising. But it changed hockey forever by making it popular in new places. Hockey had always been popular in Canada. Now people in Hollywood liked it, too. The United States was changing. People were moving from states such as Pennsylvania and Ohio to states such as Arizona and California to find work. Soon, the NHL would put teams in those warm-weather places for the fans who moved there. Because of players like Gretzky, people all over the country wanted to be part of the excitement of pro hockey.

FLORIDA PANTHERS

Franchise Record: 617–677–142–138
Home Rink: BB&T Center (19,250 capacity) in Sunrise, Florida

STANLEY CUPS
None

First Season: 1993–1994

To say that the Panthers burst onto the NHL scene would be an understatement. The expansion team from south Florida was the most successful first-year team in league history, winning 33 games and compiling 83 points for the Atlantic Division standings in 1993–1994. Two years later the Panthers were competing for the Stanley Cup.

Jay Bouwmeester (4) was selected to the 2007 and 2009 All-Star games.

Legends & Stars

Nathan Horton

Pavel Bure	RW	1998–2002	Led the NHL in goals twice—both times as a Panther
Nathan Horton	C	2003–2010	No. 3 overall draft pick in 2003
John Vanbiesbrouck	G	1993–1998	1986 Vezina Trophy winner's three All-Star seasons were in Florida
Stephen Weiss	C	2001–2013	No. 4 overall draft pick in 2001

By the Numbers

TOP GOAL SCORER	**Olli Jokinen** 2000–2009 188 goals	**TOP GOALTENDER**	**Roberto Luongo** 2000–2006, 2013-present 114 wins
TOP ASSISTS MAN	**Stephen Weiss** 2001–2013 249 assists	**TOP DEFENSEMAN**	**Robert Svehla** 1994–2002 290 points

Tough Out

The Panthers were swept by the Colorado Avalanche in the 1996 Stanley Cup finals, but they didn't go down without a fight. Game 4 was scoreless into the third overtime before the Avs scored to clinch the title.

Rat Trick

On opening night of the 1995-1996 season, a rat scurried across the floor of the Panthers' locker room. Forward Scott Mellanby killed it with a slap shot against the wall. That night Mellanby scored two goals, and goalie John Vanbiesbrouck proclaimed it hockey's first "rat trick." The legend was born. As the season went on, fans threw rubber rats on the ice after Florida's first goal of a game. By the time the Stanley Cup finals came along, more than 2,000 fake rats were thrown onto the ice each game.

LOS ANGELES KINGS

First Season: 1967–1968

Franchise Record: 1,455–1,577–424–98
Home Rink: Staples Center
(18,118 capacity) in Los Angeles, California

STANLEY CUP
2012, 2014

Kings goalie Jonathan Quick makes a save against the Boston Bruins in 2010.

The NHL's "Original Six" teams resided in cold-weather cities. But when the league made its first big expansion, it went to sunny southern California, and the Los Angeles Kings were born. The team has boasted electric offensive players, including Marcel Dionne and Wayne Gretzky. As a No. 8 seed in the 2011–2012 playoffs, the Kings won the first of two Stanley Cups.

Legends & Stars

Drew Doughty

Rob Blake	D	1989–2001, 2006–2008	Norris Trophy winner in 1998
Marcel Dionne	C	1975–1987	Ranks fifth on the NHL's all-time scoring list
Drew Doughty	D	2008–present	Second overall draft pick in 2008 and All-Rookie Team pick in 2009
Wayne Gretzky	C	1988–1996	"The Great One" led the NHL in scoring and won one Hart Trophy as a King
Luc Robitaille	LW	1986–2001, 2003–2006	Eight-time All-Star Game pick and Calder Trophy winner
Jonathan Quick	G	2007–present	Won the Conn Smythe Trophy as playoff MVP in 2012

By the Numbers

TOP GOAL SCORER — Luc Robitaille
1986–2001, 2003–2006
557 goals

TOP ASSISTS MAN — Marcel Dionne
1975–1987
757 assists

TOP GOALTENDER — Jonathan Quick
2007–present
176 wins

TOP DEFENSEMAN — Rob Blake
1989–2001, 2006–2008
494 points

Down but Not Out

Six years before getting "The Great One," the Kings pulled off the unthinkable. They eliminated Gretzky's Oilers from the Stanley Cup playoffs. The series win included a stunning, come-from-behind victory. The Kings were down 5-0 after two periods, but they came back to win 6-5 in overtime.

Trade of the Century

August 9, 1988, is a date that changed the NHL forever. That's when the Edmonton Oilers traded the game's greatest player, Wayne Gretzky, to the Los Angeles Kings. Number 99—now retired by the entire league—played to sellout crowds every night. He led L.A. to its only Stanley Cup finals appearance. After winning four times with the Oilers, however, he couldn't clinch one for the Kings.

Each Kings player wore Gretzky's 99 as a tribute after his number was retired.

MINNESOTA WILD

First Season: 2000–2001

Franchise Record: 474-408-55-95
Home Rink: Xcel Energy Center
(18,064 capacity) in St. Paul, Minnesota

STANLEY CUPS
None

Minnesota is the self-proclaimed "State of Hockey." But after the North Stars left for Dallas in 1993, the state was without an NHL team for seven years. When the league expanded for the last time, it was only natural to go back to a hockey-crazy part of the United States. In 2010 the team played in its 400th home game. Every one of those games was played before a sellout crowd, the third-longest sellout streak in NHL history.

Wild center Wes Walz spent seven seasons in Minnesota.

Legends & Stars

Mikko Koivu

Niklas Backstrom	G	2006–present	Jennings Trophy winner in 2007
Marian Gaborik	RW	2000–2009	Two-time All-Star Game selection
Mikko Koivu	C	2005–present	Wild captain was a first-round draft pick in 2001
Zach Parise	LW	2012–present	Led Wild in goals and points during first season
Ryan Suter	D	2012–present	Led NHL in minutes played per game in 2013

By the Numbers

TOP GOAL SCORER — Marian Gaborik — 2000–2009 — 219 goals

TOP GOALTENDER — Niklas Backstrom — 2006–present — 189 wins

TOP ASSISTS MAN — Mikko Koivu — 2005–present — 322 assists

TOP DEFENSEMAN — Brent Burns — 2003–2011 — 183 points

Playoff Run

In just its third season in the NHL, the Wild made a playoff charge all the way to the Western Conference finals. The unlikely run included overtime victories in Games 6 and 7 against the favored Colorado Avalanche. Andrew Brunette's series-winning goal not only led his team to the second round, it also ended the career of goaltending great Patrick Roy, who retired after the season.

Popular Pair

The Minnesota Wild set off fireworks in the hockey world when they signed two of the NHL's biggest stars to long-term contracts July 4, 2012. Forward Zach Parise and defenseman Ryan Suter instantly brought dreams of winning a Stanley Cup to Wild fans. Parise's dad, J.P., played nine seasons for the Minnesota North Stars and was a two-time All-Star.

Zach Parise joined the Wild in 2012.

MONTREAL CANADIENS

First Season: 1917–1918

Franchise Record: 3,210–2,094–837–109
Home Rink: **Bell Centre** (21,273 capacity) in Montreal, Quebec, Canada

STANLEY CUPS
1916, 1924, 1930, 1931, 1944, 1946, 1953, 1956, 1957, 1958, 1959, 1960, 1965, 1966, 1968, 1969, 1971, 1973, 1976, 1977, 1978, 1979, 1986, 1993

When it comes to winning, few sports teams have had the success of the Montreal Canadiens. With 24 Stanley Cup victories, only Major League Baseball's New York Yankees have won more championships (27). Twice, the nearly century-old hockey club won four titles in a row, a feat accomplished just one other time in NHL history.

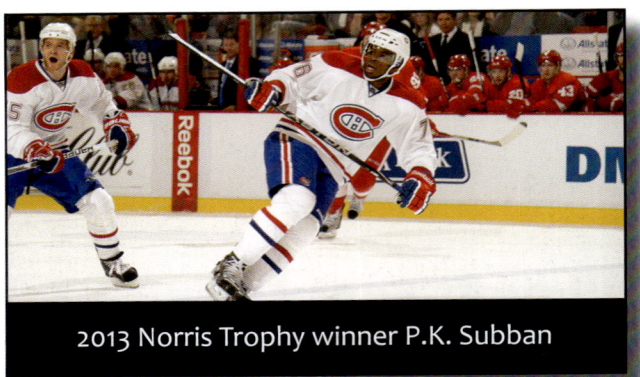
2013 Norris Trophy winner P.K. Subban

Legends & Stars

Jacques Plante

Name	Pos	Years	Notes
Jean Beliveau	C	1950–1951, 1952–1971	Won 10 Stanley Cups, including five as team captain
Hector "Toe" Blake		1955–1968	Montreal coach led Canadiens to eight championships
Scotty Bowman		1971–1979	Canadiens coach won five of his nine Stanley Cups with Montreal
Ken Dryden	G	1970–1979	Won the Calder and Conn Smythe trophies as a rookie
Doug Harvey	D	1947–1961	Seven-time Norris Trophy winner
Guy Lafleur	RW	1971–1985	Led the league in scoring three times; won five Cups
Howie Morenz	C	1923–1934, 1936–1937	One of the NHL's first stars was a three-time Hart Trophy winner
Jacques Plante	G	1952–1963	Seven-time Vezina Trophy winner was the first goalie to wear a mask
Carey Price	C	2007–present	First-round draft pick was the All-Rookie Team goalie in 2008
Maurice Richard	RW	1942–1960	"Rocket" led the Canadiens to eight Stanley Cup victories
Larry Robinson	D	1972–1989	Conn Smythe Trophy winner in 1976

By the Numbers

 **TOP GOAL SCORER** — Maurice Richard 1942–1960 544 goals

 **TOP GOALTENDER** — Jacques Plante 1952–1963 314 wins

 **TOP ASSISTS MAN** — Guy Lafleur 1971–1985 728 assists

 **TOP DEFENSEMAN** — Larry Robinson 1972–1989 883 points

Riot for the Rocket

Maurice "Rocket" Richard, a fan favorite, was suspended for the rest of the 1955 season after injuring an opposing player and punching an official. After learning about Richard's suspension, people rioted in the streets of Montreal, causing $500,000 in damage. In 1957 Richard became the NHL's first 500-goal scorer.

Maurice Richard scores against Red Wings goalie Terry Sawchuk during a 1954 game.

The Canadiens' Cup

With 24 championships, the Stanley Cup has belonged to Montreal for nearly a quarter of its history. Jean Beliveau has his name on the Cup 17 times—10 as a player and 7 as a team executive. Henri Richard, brother of Maurice Richard, won it 11 times as a player—more than any other. Yvan Cournoyer also has his name on it 10 times.

GREAT TEAMS IN FOCUS

1955-1956 MONTREAL CANADIENS

The 1950s saw Montreal dominate the NHL like no team had ever done before. Maurice Richard was a hero to people who spoke both French and English. Forwards such as Bernie "Boom-Boom" Geoffrion, who invented the slapshot, and Jean Beliveau, who led the league in scoring, became fan favorites. With Doug Harvey on defense and Jacques Plante in goal, the Canadiens won five straight Stanley Cups.

The 1955–1956 Canadiens were a great team that featured 12 future Hockey Hall of Fame players, including manager Frank Selke and coach Toe Blake. During the regular season, Beliveau won the scoring title with 47 goals, earning the Art Ross Trophy for leading goal-scorer. He also set a record for most goals and assists as a center. Bert Olmstead, the team's left wing, also set a record with 56 assists.

The Canadiens were so talented on the power play that they forced a rule change. Previously, players would serve the full two minutes of their penalty. Montreal scored so often, this rule was changed to end the penalty after a goal was scored against the other team. Richard was at his best, scoring 38 goals. The Canadiens had a fantastic goalie in Jacques "Jake the Snake" Plante. He was the first modern goaltender. He left the net to play the puck and charge shooters instead of waiting for them to shoot. Plante won five straight Vezina trophies as the best goalie in the league and had two shutouts in the 1956 playoffs.

Toe Blake coached the Canadiens during the 1955–1956 season.

70

Great Teams in Focus

Jean Beliveau (1931-)

Jean Beliveau was among the league's leading scorers for two decades and was team captain during some of the Canadiens' greatest years. He retired after the Canadiens won the Cup in 1971 and became the first player to skate a lap of the ice with the trophy. After his retirement, Beliveau was often urged to run for political office. In 1994 he was asked to become governor general of Canada, which was a great honor. Beliveau said no, out of modesty. In 2003, when Montreal fans booed the U.S. anthem in protest of the war in Iraq, the team played a videotaped message from Beliveau. No one booed after that.

GREAT TEAMS IN FOCUS

Montreal ended the 1955–1956 regular season with a 24-point lead over the nearest opponent, the second-placed Red Wings. In the semifinals of the playoffs, the Canadiens faced the New York Rangers. The Canadiens won the series 4–1 and advanced to the Stanley Cup finals for the second straight year. In the other semifinal series, Detroit beat Toronto 4–1, setting up a rematch of the previous year's finals.

In Game 1 of the finals, the Red Wings played better for the first two periods. Montreal came back in the third period behind goals from Beliveau, Geoffrion, and Claude Provost and ended up winning 6–4. The Canadiens continued to score a lot of goals in Game 2 and beat Detroit 5–1. Detroit, the defending champions, would not be pushed around, though. In Game 3, behind goals from Red Kelly, Ted Lindsay, and Gordie Howe, the Red Wings won 3–1, bringing the series to 2–1.

The defense of the Canadiens was outstanding in Game 4. Beliveau scored two goals and Floyd Curry added one to lead their team to a 3–0 victory. Montreal was now up 3–1 and was only one victory away from the Stanley Cup. They wanted the championship badly and won the next game 4–1 to take the Cup. Beliveau and Geoffrion continued their great offensive play, each scoring a goal in the game. In the playoffs, Beliveau scored an amazing 12 goals, two being game winners, and had seven assists. He finished the season with a total of 59 goals. The Canadiens were not finished there. They went on to win the Stanley Cup for the next four seasons, stretching out their championship run to five years!

HISTORY BOX
CARRYING THE FLAG

English-speaking colonists and immigrants settled most of Canada, but the French settled the area that is now Quebec. Quebec is very proud of its language and traditions, and the Canadiens are extremely popular there. The team is fondly known as "The Habs," short for "Les Habitants." This is a French term meaning "the country boys" or "the local boys." Local players such as Richard, Beliveau, and Guy Lafleur are heroes there to this day.

1955-1956 Montreal Canadiens

1955-1956 Record

Won	Lost	Tied	Playoffs
45	15	10	Defeated New York Rangers 4–1
			Defeated Detroit Red Wings 4–1

The Montreal Canadiens' coach is hoisted into the air to celebrate their victory over the Red Wings.

GREAT TEAMS IN FOCUS

1976-1977 MONTREAL CANADIENS

The greatest dynasty the hockey world has known was the Montreal Canadiens of the mid- to late 1960s and 1970s. The team truly earned their nickname—"Les Glorieux," or "The Glorious." The Canadiens won 10 Cups in 15 years.

Montreal's best team was the 1976–1977 squad that won the Stanley Cup that season. They won a league high of 60 games and had only eight losses! The way the Canadiens played changed the game. They scored a lot of goals, but concentrated on defense. The Canadiens had nine future Hall of Famers on the roster: Ken Dryden in goal, with Guy Lapointe, Larry Robinson, and Serge Savard on defense. Jacques Lemaire and Bob Gainey were center or played center, and Guy Lafleur, Yvan Cournoyer, and Steve Schutt were on the wings. Sam Pollack was the general manager, and Scotty Bowman was the coach. Both Pollack and Bowman are also in the Hall of Fame.

Ken Dryden (1947-)

In 1971 Canadiens coach Scotty Bowman picked a rookie goalie named Ken Dryden as his playoff starter. Dryden had played in only six NHL games, but the Canadiens won the Cup. Dryden was named Rookie of the Year the next season. Dryden was more than a goalie. He sat out the 1973–1974 season to attend law school. He also wrote a book called *The Game*, which is considered one of the finest books about hockey. Dryden's hockey career was short, but brilliant. In eight seasons he won the Vezina Trophy as best goalie five times, the Conn Smythe Trophy as playoff MVP twice, and played on six Stanley Cup–winning teams.

Great Teams in Focus

Lafleur led the league in scoring with 136 points, and Schutt led the league in goals with 60, a record for a left wing. The Canadiens had 132 points in 80 games—a record that hasn't been broken. They lost only once at their home arena, the Forum. This defeat was to the Bruins, early in the year. However, the Canadiens got a chance for revenge in the Stanley Cup finals.

Montreal's Guy Lafleur (center, in white) battles for the puck against the Cleveland Barons.

GREAT TEAMS IN FOCUS

The Canadiens were just as dominant in the first two rounds of the playoffs as they were in the regular season. They swept St. Louis and beat the Islanders to advance to the Cup finals. They met the Boston Bruins in the championship.

The Canadiens showed that they wanted the championship by scoring two goals in the first five minutes against the Bruins in Game 1. They took only 24 shots all game, but an unbelievable seven of those shots got past Boston's goalie, Gerry Cheevers. The Canadiens dominated and won 7–3. Yvon Lambert and Mario Tremblay each scored two goals for Montreal. As in Game 1, Montreal took very few shots on goal in Game 2. They shot only 19 times, but three shots were for goals. Schutt was Montreal's offensive hero, scoring a goal and assisting on two. Canadiens goalie Dryden blocked all 21 shots he faced, as Montreal shut out the Bruins 3–0. They now held a 2–0 series lead.

Montreal player Serge Savard lifts the Stanley Cup above his head to celebrate the championship.

1976–1977 Montreal Canadiens

1976–1977 Record

Won	Lost	Tied	Playoffs
60	8	12	Defeated St. Louis Blues 4–0
			Defeated New York Islanders 4–2
			Defeated Boston Bruins 4–0

In Game 3, the Canadiens continued to dominate. In the first period they took only six shots, but three went in! The Bruins could not stop them, and the Canadiens won 4–2. Facing a sweep in Game 4, the Bruins came out fighting. They got their first lead of the entire series on a goal from Bobby Schmautz, but the Canadiens came right back to tie in the second period. No team scored again, so the game went into overtime. Although it was the best game the Bruins had played all series, they were just no match for Montreal. Four minutes into overtime, Lemaire scored, on an assist from Lafleur, for the game- and Cup-winning goal. The victory gave the Canadiens their 20th Stanley Cup. Lafleur, who led the playoffs in scoring with 26 points, received the Conn Smythe Trophy, given to the most outstanding player in the playoffs.

No team that came before dominated the game the way the Canadiens did. They won an amazing 12 of 14 games in the playoffs. No team that came after had as much pure talent as that team. There would be great players, such as Wayne Gretzky and Mario Lemieux, in the years to come, but no team ever won as easily as the Canadiens did in 1977.

HISTORY BOX

SPENDING TIME WITH THE CUP

Guy Lafleur scored many goals in 1976–1977, but one of the biggest in his career came during the 1979 Stanley Cup finals. He scored late in the third period of Game 7 to tie the game. The Canadiens won the game and the Cup in overtime. While his teammates celebrated that night, Lafleur stole the Cup from the trunk of a car. He showed it off on the lawn of his home. He escaped punishment only because of his popularity. Today, every player on the winning team gets to spend a day with the Cup.

NASHVILLE PREDATORS

First Season: 1998–1999

Franchise Record: 557-479-60-100
Home Rink: Bridgestone Arena (17,113 capacity) in Nashville, Tennessee

STANLEY CUPS
None

In 1971 construction workers in downtown Nashville discovered an underground cave. A 9-inch (23-centimeter) fang and a leg bone of a saber-toothed tiger were found in the cave. Nearly 30 years later, the NHL arrived in Tennessee. Instead of naming the new team after Nashville's famous country-music scene, it was called the Predators and the logo became an ancient tiger.

Predators goalie Pekka Rinne had seven shutouts during the 2009–2010 season.

Legends & Stars

Tomas Vokoun

Name	Pos	Years	Notes
Jason Arnott	C	2006–2010	Went to the All-Star Game in 2008 as a Predator
Steve Sullivan	RW	2004–2011	Bill Masterton Trophy winner in 2009
Tomas Vokoun	G	1998–2007	Named to the All-Star Game twice as a Predator
Shea Weber	D	2005–present	Nashville defenseman is a three-time All-Star

By the Numbers

TOP GOAL SCORER
David Legwand
1998–2014
210 goals

TOP GOALTENDER
Pekka Rinne
2005–present
163 wins

TOP ASSISTS MAN
David Legwand
356 assists

TOP DEFENSEMAN
Shea Weber
2005–present
347 points

Perfect Marriage

Many expansion teams go through several coaches and managers before getting things right. Not Nashville. For the first 15 seasons of the Predators' existence, general manager David Poile and head coach Barry Trotz ran the team.

Predators coach Barry Trotz (left)

Historic Skate

On opening night of the 2003–2004 season, Predators rookie Jordin Tootoo became the first player of Inuit descent to appear in an NHL game. Tootoo was raised in Rankin Inlet, Nunavut, in northern Canada. Tootoo played five seasons in the NHL, all with Nashville, and had 26 goals and 35 assists.

NEW JERSEY DEVILS

First Season: 1974–1975

Franchise Record: 1,314–1,361–328–95
Home Rink: Prudential Center
(17,625 capacity) in Newark, New Jersey

STANLEY CUPS
1995, 2000, 2003

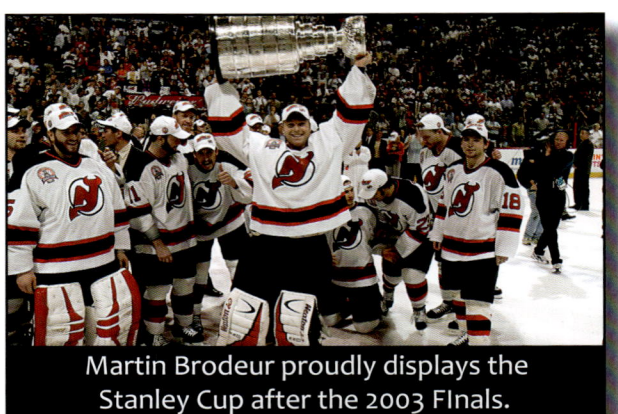
Martin Brodeur proudly displays the Stanley Cup after the 2003 Finals.

The Devils started out in the Midwest as the Kansas City Scouts. Two years later, in 1976, they moved west and became the Colorado Rockies. But the team finally found a home on the East Coast in 1982. In New Jersey the team enjoyed its first winning season, its first playoff series win, and three Stanley Cup championships.

Legends & Stars

Patrik Elias

Martin Brodeur	G	1991–2014	Won five Jennings Trophys and four Vezina Trophys
Ken Daneyko	D	1983–2003	Played in a team-record 1,283 games over 20 seasons
Claude Lemieux	F	1990–1995	Conn Smythe Trophy winner in 1995
Zach Parise	LW	2005–2012	High-scoring forward earned an All-Star selection in 2009
Scott Stevens	D	1991–2004	Tough body checker led the Devils to three titles
Patrik Elias	C	1995–present	Three-time All-Star is Devils' all-time leading scorer

By the Numbers

 **Patrik Elias**
1995–present
393 goals
590 assists

 **Patrik Elias**
555 assists

 **Martin Brodeur**
1991–2014
688 wins

 **Scott Niedermayer**
1991–2004
476 points

All-Time Winner

In 2009 the Devils' Martin Brodeur won his 552nd game, passing Patrick Roy. The next season, he reached 104 career shutouts and passed Terry Sawchuk's record. But he wasn't done yet. Through the 2013–2014 season, Brodeur had won 688 games and earned 124 shutouts, all with the Devils.

Devils goalie Martin Brodeur

Comeback Kids

To win the 2000 Stanley Cup, the Devils did something no other team had done. They were down three games to one in the conference finals, but they came back to beat the Flyers. They went on to defeat the Stars for the title.

NEW YORK ISLANDERS

First Season: 1972–1973

Franchise Record: 1,405–1,399–347–103
Home Rink: Nassau Veterans Memorial Coliseum (16,234 capacity) in Uniondale, New York

STANLEY CUPS
1980, 1981, 1982, 1983

The New York Islanders were the best team of the early 1980s, winning four consecutive Stanley Cups. (Turn the page to learn more about their amazing 1981–1982 season.) Only one other franchise in NHL history had ever accomplished that feat—the Montreal Canadiens did it twice. In 2015 the Islanders will move from Long Island to the New York City borough of Brooklyn.

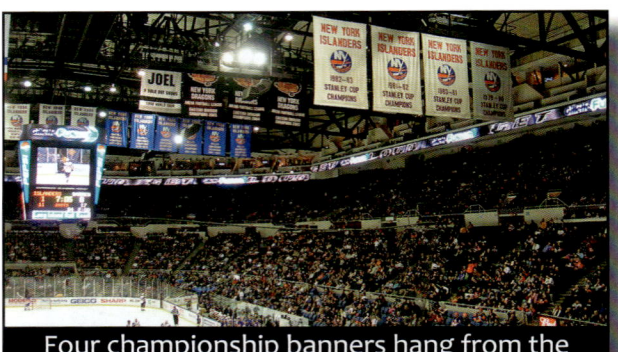
Four championship banners hang from the rafters in Veterans Memorial Coliseum.

Legends & Stars

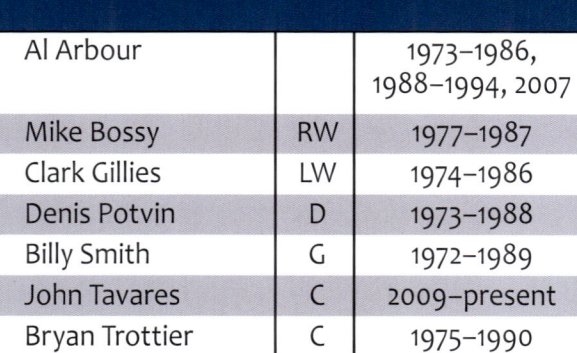

Bryan Trottier

Name	Position	Years	Notes
Al Arbour		1973–1986, 1988–1994, 2007	Coached New York's four championship teams
Mike Bossy	RW	1977–1987	Scored a record 53 goals as a rookie
Clark Gillies	LW	1974–1986	Scored 30 or more goals in six different seasons
Denis Potvin	D	1973–1988	Captain of the Islanders' four title teams
Billy Smith	G	1972–1989	Conn Smythe Trophy winner in 1983
John Tavares	C	2009–present	No. 1 overall draft pick in 2009 and 2012 All-Star
Bryan Trottier	C	1975–1990	Retired as the NHL's sixth all-time leading scorer

By the Numbers

TOP GOAL SCORER	Mike Bossy 1977–1987 573 goals	**TOP GOALTENDER**	Billy Smith 1972–1989 304 wins
TOP ASSISTS MAN	Bryan Trottier 1975–1990 853 assists	**TOP DEFENSEMAN**	Denis Potvin 1973–1988 1052 points

Working Overtime

On their way to their first Stanley Cup, the Islanders won six of seven overtime games in the playoffs. That included Game 6 of the finals against the Philadelphia Flyers. Bob Nystrom scored the game-winning goal to give the Islanders the championship.

Bob Nystrom

Easter Epic

In 1987 the Isles won a playoff game that started on a Saturday night in April and didn't end until early Easter Sunday morning. New York's Pat LaFontaine scored during the fourth overtime to clinch the victory. It was the NHL's first four-overtime game in 36 years.

GREAT TEAMS IN FOCUS

1981-1982 NEW YORK ISLANDERS

Playing on Long Island in the New York City suburbs, the Islanders were a rare team: they were a team without a city. The Islanders' fans considered them New Yorkers at heart, but they had to come from all over Long Island to cheer on their team against the New York Rangers.

The Islanders had powerful forwards such as Bryan Trottier, Mike Bossy, and Clark Gillies, and a great defenseman in Denis Potvin. In the net Billy Smith used his stick to stop pucks and hack at the ankles of any player who got near him. In 1982 the Islanders were at their best, winning their third of four straight Stanley Cups. They led the NHL in wins during the regular season, at one point setting a record with 15 straight wins. The Islanders went into the playoffs as favorites to win the Cup.

Islanders' player Denis Potvin waits for the puck.

Great Teams in Focus

However, the first round didn't go as smoothly as they might have liked. They faced a tough Pittsburgh Penguins team. The Islanders started the series strong, winning the first two games. But then they didn't play as well and lost the next two games. The series was tied at 2–2, and it all came down to Game 5. It was a great game. The Islanders were down one goal with only 2:21 remaining when John Tonelli scored a goal and forced overtime. Tonelli continued his heroic play in overtime and scored the game winner, sending his team to the next round.

HISTORY BOX

RIVAL LEAGUES MERGE

After decades in which there were only six pro hockey teams, the 1970s saw the sport change with the NHL's growth to 20 teams. There was also a new league. The World Hockey Association (WHA) was founded in 1972 with 12 teams. Bobby Hull was the first NHL star to sign with the rival association for the then-amazing sum of $1 million! While the NHL had a defensive game, the WHA was all about offense. The WHA collapsed in 1979, and four teams—Edmonton, Hartford, Quebec, and Winnipeg—were invited to join the established league. The Islanders beat Quebec on their way to the Stanley Cup in 1982.

The Islanders won four straight Stanley Cups between 1979 and 1983.

GREAT TEAMS IN FOCUS

1981-1982 Record

Won	Lost	Tied	Playoffs
54	16	10	Defeated Pittsburgh Penguins 3–2
			Defeated New York Rangers 4–2
			Defeated Quebec Nordiques 4–0
			Defeated Vancouver Canucks 4–0

The Islanders then beat the New York Rangers in six games and swept the Quebec Nordiques to advance to the Stanley Cup finals against the Vancouver Canucks. However, in Game 1, the Canucks played great and led 5–4 with only seven minutes remaining in the game. Their lead didn't last long against the great Islanders. Bossy scored a goal to tie the game at 5–5 with less than five minutes to play. Neither team scored again, and the game went into overtime. Both teams played great defense in overtime, and it looked as if the game would be sent to double overtime. But with only two seconds left, Bossy scored another goal to steal the win. Vancouver came out strong again in Game 2, holding onto a slim 3–2 lead going into the final period. New York came back, scoring two quick goals to take back the lead, 4–3. The Islanders never looked back, scoring two more goals for a 6–4 win and 2–0 series lead.

New York dominated both offensively and defensively in Game 3. They shut out the Canucks, as Gillies, Bob Nystrom, and Bossy all scored goals for a 3–0 victory and 3–0 series lead. The Islanders were only one game away from a sweep and Stanley Cup trophy.

The Canucks didn't want to be swept in the finals, but there wasn't much they could do to stop the Islanders. Bossy proved that he was a great playoff player as he scored two goals in the game. The Canucks never threatened the Islanders as New York won 4–0, earning the Cup and sweeping their opponent. Bossy's 17 post-season goals led to his winning the Conn Smythe Trophy.

1981-1982 New York Islanders

Mike Bossy (1957-)

In 1982 Mike Bossy scored one of the most memorable goals in Stanley Cup history. Shoved away from the net by an opposing player, Bossy managed to get his stick on the puck as he fell. With both feet in the air, he fired a backhand into the net. Bossy had a gift for scoring, and it served him well. He is still the only player in NHL history with nine straight 50-goal seasons. Bossy was important for another reason. He didn't like fighting because other players had beat him up when he was young. At the time that Bossy played, fighting was a big part of hockey. Thanks to players like Bossy, the NHL became less violent.

NEW YORK RANGERS

First Season: 1926–1927

Franchise Record: 2,606–2,513–808–97
Home Rink: Madison Square Garden (18,200 capacity) in New York, New York

STANLEY CUPS
1928, 1933, 1940, 1994

The Rangers weren't the first NHL team to play at Madison Square Garden, but they were the survivors. In 1926 the New York Americans also called Manhattan home. But the Rangers, nicknamed the Blueshirts, quickly became the top team in the league. They earned the best record in the league in their first year and clinched the Stanley Cup in their second.

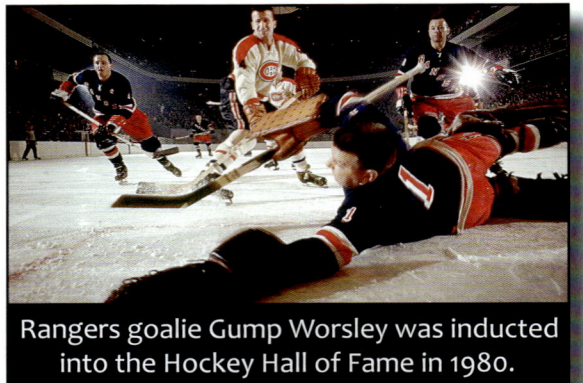
Rangers goalie Gump Worsley was inducted into the Hockey Hall of Fame in 1980.

Legends & Stars

Henrik Lundqvist

Andy Bathgate	RW	1952–1964	NHL's MVP in 1959
Frank Boucher	C	1926–1938, 1943–1944	Seven-time Lady Byng Trophy winner
Bill Cook	RW	1926–1937	Captain of the Rangers' first two championship teams
Brian Leetch	D	1987–2003	Won two Norris trophies and the Conn Smythe in 1994
Henrik Lundqvist	G	2005–present	Three-time All-Star captured the Vezina Trophy in 2012
Brad Park	D	1968–1975	Named to nine All-Star Games in 17 seasons
Lester Patrick		1926–1939	The Rangers' first coach won two Stanley Cups

By the Numbers

Top Goal Scorer
Rod Gilbert
1960–1978
406 goals

Top Assists Man
Brian Leetch
1987–2003
741 assists

Top Goaltender
Henrik Lundqvist
2005–present
301 wins

Top Defenseman
Brian Leetch →
981 points

1940 Chant

For many years opposing fans mocked the Rangers by chanting "1940! 1940!" during playoff games. That was the last year they had won a title. But captain Mark Messier put an end to the chant in 1994, helping New York hoist the Stanley Cup again. (For more on this Cup-winning season, turn the page.)

Mark Messier was inducted into the NHL Hall of Fame in 2007.

Tex's Team

The Rangers were first organized by Madison Square Garden President G.I. "Tex" Rickard. While the team was being formed, sportswriters had fun with Rickard's nickname. They called the team "Tex's Rangers"—playing off the name of the famous lawmen, the Texas Rangers. Rickard liked the name so much he had it stitched on the team's jerseys.

89

GREAT TEAMS IN FOCUS

1993-1994 NEW YORK RANGERS

The New York Rangers were one of hockey's "Original Six." Their last Stanley Cup win came in 1940. In 1993 the Rangers turned to a fiery coach named Mike Keenan. He had taken two teams to the Stanley Cup finals, but players didn't like his harsh methods. The Rangers had talent, but they didn't work very hard as a team. Keenan changed that. He was known for getting his players in shape.

The Rangers didn't even make the playoffs in 1992–1993, but Keenan came in and told his players that his goal for them was to win the Stanley Cup. The players believed that they could do it. Keenan hung a picture of the Stanley Cup in their locker room so that the players would be reminded of what they were playing for.

The Rangers had three great players. Mark Messier was the captain and leader. The Rangers had gotten Messier from the Edmonton Oilers, as well as Adam Graves. Messier had won championships in Edmonton, and his teammates listened to him and respected him, knowing that he could help them win a championship. Brian Leetch was one of the game's best young defensemen, as was rookie Sergei Zubov. The Rangers also had a young goalie named Mike Richter who was ready to become a star. Richter had spent time in the minor leagues the previous year, but he showed he could play at the professional level. He won a league-high 42 games during the regular season!

The Rangers started out the season 4–5. They were very frustrated, and coach Keenan was very angry and disappointed with his team. Keenan motivated his team, and they won 12 out of their next 14 games. They moved into first place and never looked back. They were in first place the rest of the season.

HISTORY BOX

LOCKOUT!

In April 1992, NHL players staged a brief 30-game strike to protest working conditions. That dispute was solved in time for the playoffs. In the fall of 1994, when the agreement expired, NHL owners shut down the league when a new deal couldn't be reached. The season's start was delayed until January, as players wanted more freedom of movement and owners wanted to put a stop to huge increases in salaries. The 105-day lockout couldn't have come at a worse time for the NHL. The Rangers' win captured the attention of both New York and the nation, and hockey was labeled a "hot" sport. The lockout didn't solve much—a decade later, in 2004, and then again in 2012–2013, the owners once again locked out the players.

Great Teams in Focus

Mike Keenan (1949-)

Mike Keenan's tough rules brought the best out of his players. He went to the Stanley Cup finals three times with the Blackhawks and Flyers, but he left both teams when he couldn't get along with his bosses. He was in New York less than a month in the fall of 1993 when he smashed a stick on the goal during practice. The Rangers got the message and went on to finish first overall and win the Cup. During the summer, Keenan argued with general manager Neil Smith and jumped to the St. Louis Blues to take on the dual roles of general manager and coach.

GREAT TEAMS IN FOCUS

1993-1994 Record

Won	Lost	Tied	Playoffs
52	24	8	Defeated New York Islanders 4–0
			Defeated Washington Capitals 4–1
			Defeated New Jersey Devils 4–3

In the first round of the playoffs, the Rangers swept their rivals, the Islanders, outscoring them 22–3. In the second round, they faced the Washington Capitals, beating them four games to one.

In the conference finals, the Rangers met their rivals from across the Hudson River, the New Jersey Devils. The Devils hadn't beaten the Rangers in six regular season games, but it wasn't the regular season anymore. It was a great series full of big goals and big saves. The series had three double-overtime games! The Devils led the series after Game 5, but Messier had something to say. Before Game 6, he guaranteed the Rangers would win. He made sure they did—by scoring a hat trick! The Rangers won Game 7 in double overtime and advanced to the Cup finals.

Rangers captain Mark Messier skates during a game against the New Jersey Devils.

1993-1994 New York Rangers

Mark Messier looks for the puck in a game against the Montreal Canadiens.

In the finals, the Vancouver Canucks gave the Rangers everything they could handle. The Rangers started out the series playing great, winning three games and losing only one. The Canucks came back and won Game 5 with a score of 6–3. The Rangers had a chance to win the series in Game 6, but Vancouver won at home 4–1, sending the series back to Madison Square Garden for Game 7. Messier scored to give the Rangers a 3–1 lead, but Vancouver scored in the third period to get within a goal. The Canucks attacked and attacked, but the Rangers held on for their first Stanley Cup in 54 years. In 2004 *The Hockey News* voted it the best Cup final of all time.

OTTAWA SENATORS

First Season: 1992–1993

Franchise Record: 741–699–115–103
Home Rink: Scotiabank Place (20,004 capacity) in Ottawa, Ontario, Canada

STANLEY CUPS
None

For the first 34 years of the 1900s, the Ottawa Senators played professional hockey and even won the Stanley Cup. But the team folded in 1934, leaving Canada's hockey-hungry capital city without an NHL team for almost 60 years. When the league expanded in 1992, a new team with an old name was formed.

Senators goalie Brian Elliott

Legends & Stars

Dany Heatley

Craig Anderson	G	2011–present	Led the NHL with a .941 save percentage in 2013
Daniel Alfredsson	RW	1995–2013	Calder Trophy winner in 1996 and six-time All Star
Dany Heatley	LW	2003–2009	Had two 100-point seasons for the Senators
Jason Spezza	C	2002–2014	Drafted second overall in 2001

By the Numbers

TOP GOAL SCORER
Daniel Alfredsson
1995–2013
426 goals

TOP ASSISTS MAN
Daniel Alfredsson
682 assists

TOP GOALTENDER
Patrick Lalime
1999–2004
146 wins

TOP DEFENSEMAN
Wade Redden
1996–2008
410 points

Captain Dan

For 17 years, Daniel Alfredsson was the face of the franchise. He was drafted in 1994, joined the team in 1995, and received the captain's "C" in 1999. He also scored the overtime game-winning goal to put Ottawa into the Stanley Cup finals in 2007. They ended up losing the series to the Anaheim Ducks.

Daniel Alfredsson (11)

Tribute to the Past

During their franchise-opening game, the Senators paid tribute to the city's original team. They retired the number 8, the jersey number of Frank Finnigan. He led the old Senators to a 1927 Stanley Cup championship. In his later years, Finnigan campaigned to bring the NHL back to Ottawa.

PHILADELPHIA FLYERS

Franchise Record: 1,821–1,254–457–104
Home Rink: Wells Fargo Center (19,519 capacity) in Philadelphia, Pennsylvania

STANLEY CUPS
1974, 1975

First Season: 1967–1968

In 1967 the NHL expanded from six teams to 12, adding franchises in California, Minnesota, Missouri, and Pennsylvania. One of those Pennsylvania teams, the Philadelphia Flyers, became the first of the new teams to win the Stanley Cup. They won back-to-back titles in their flashy, orange sweaters in the mid-1970s.

The Philadelphia Flyers took on the Boston Bruins in the 2010 NHL Winter Classic.

Legends & Stars

Simon Gagne

Bill Barber	LW	1972–1984	Played in six All-Star Games
Bobby Clarke	C	1969–1984	Three-time Hart Trophy winner
Simon Gagne	LW	1999–2010	All-Rookie in 2000 and two-time All-Star Game pick
Claude Giroux	RW	2007–present	Two-time All-Star collected 93 points in 2011–2012
Eric Lindros	C	1992–2000	Hart Trophy winner in 1995
Bernie Parent	G	1967–1971, 1973–1979	Conn Smythe Trophy winner in each Stanley Cup run
Fred Shero		1971–1978	Coached the Flyers to their two championships

By the Numbers

TOP GOAL SCORER	**Bill Barber** 1972–1984 420 goals	**TOP GOALTENDER**	**Ron Hextall** 1986–1992, 1994–1999 240 wins
TOP ASSISTS MAN	**Bobby Clarke** 1969–1984 852 assists	**TOP DEFENSEMAN**	**Mark Howe** 1982–1992 480 points

Broad Street Bullies

There wasn't anything fancy about the Flyers' title teams. Captain Bobby Clarke's squad knew how to win ugly games, often intimidating and fighting their opponents. Since their home arena, the Spectrum, was located on Broad Street, the feisty team was given the nickname the Broad Street Bullies.

Flyers left wing Dave Schultz (left) makes a hard check in the 1974 NHL Finals.

Hextall Shoots and Scores

Goaltender Ron Hextall did a lot more than stop pucks. He was considered one of the best puck-handling and passing goalies in the league. On December 8, 1987, Hextall did something no other goaltender had ever done before: shoot and score a goal. It happened late in the game after the Boston Bruins had pulled their goalie for an extra skater. Hextall got the puck and fired it the length of the ice into the empty net. He did it again on April 11, 1989, becoming the first goalie to score in a playoff game.

PITTSBURGH PENGUINS

Franchise Record: 1,594–1,566–383–93
Home Rink: Consol Energy Center (18,087 capacity) in Pittsburgh, Pennsylvania

STANLEY CUPS
1991, 1992, 2009

First Season: 1967–1968

Few teams get to say they have one of the greatest players of all time in their uniform. For the Pittsburgh Penguins, it was "Super" Mario Lemieux, who led the team to back-to-back championships in the early 1990s. The Penguins are now able to boast of another star: Sidney Crosby. The young phenom took the Penguins to a title in 2009 and scored the game-winning goal for Canada in the 2010 Winter Olympics.

2009 Stanley Cup champions

Jaromir Jagr

Sidney Crosby	C	2005–present	2007 Hart Trophy winner led Penguins to their third Cup
Ron Francis	C	1991–1998	Three-time Lady Byng Trophy winner
Jaromir Jagr	RW	1990–2001	Five-time NHL scoring champion and nine-time All-Star
Mario Lemieux	C	1984–1997, 2000–2006	Three-time Hart Trophy winner; averaged 1.88 points per game
Evgeni Malkin	C	2006–present	Three-time All-Star won the Hart Trophy in 2012

By the Numbers

TOP GOAL SCORER  Mario Lemieux
1984–1997, 2000–2006
690 goals

TOP GOALTENDER  Marc-Andre Fleury
2003–present
288 wins

TOP ASSISTS MAN  Mario Lemieux
1,033 assists

TOP DEFENSEMAN  Paul Coffey
1987–1992
440 points

A Special Honor

Mario Lemieux was so good that something special happened after he retired in 1997. The Hockey Hall of Fame waived its three-year waiting period and inducted him immediately.

Sidney Crosby

Sid the Kid

Expectations were high for Sidney Crosby when he came into the NHL in 2005, but he more than exceeded them. Crosby became the youngest team captain, the youngest scoring champion, and the youngest player to reach 200 points in league history.

GREAT TEAMS IN FOCUS

1991-1992 PITTSBURGH PENGUINS

The Penguins were a last-place team when Mario Lemieux arrived in the fall of 1984. But general manager Craig Patrick went about building a team around Lemieux, and by 1992 the Pittsburgh Penguins were the best team in the NHL. With Lemieux leading the way, and stars such as Jaromir Jagr and Ron Francis helping him, the Penguins won back-to-back Cups in 1991 and 1992.

Jaromir Jagr helped the Penguins win the Stanley Cup in 1991 and 1992.

Lemieux was bigger than the great Wayne Gretzky, standing nearly 7 feet tall in skates, but he had the same skills and grasp of the game. Only untimely injuries and illness slowed him down. But it took a long time for Lemieux to become a winner. It wasn't until 1991 that the Penguins were good enough to win the Stanley Cup.

HISTORY BOX

HEAD TO HEAD

There had been other great battles for the scoring title before. Gordie Howe and Maurice Richard spent the 1950s trying to outdo each other. But the hockey world had never seen anything like the scoring race between Mario Lemieux and Wayne Gretzky fought from 1987 to 1994.

Before the 1987 season started, Gretzky had led the league for seven straight years. That year, he played in only 64 games, and Lemieux scored 70 goals to beat out Gretzky for the title, 168 points to 149. Lemieux won the next year as well, with 199 points to Gretzky's 168. The next two seasons, injuries slowed Lemieux, and Gretzky reclaimed the title. Lemieux bounced back to win in 1992–1993, and Gretzky won in 1993–1994—his last scoring title. Lemieux won two more, to give him six in his career. Gretzky won 10.

Great Teams in Focus

1991–1992 Record

Won	Lost	Tied	Playoffs
39	32	9	Defeated Washington Capitals 4–3
			Defeated New York Rangers 4–2
			Defeated Boston Bruins 4–0

While they were celebrating their 1991 Cup, tragedy struck. Coach "Badger" Bob Johnson was diagnosed with a brain tumor, and he died in November. Rallying around the memory of their lost coach, and behind new coach Scotty Bowman, the Penguins finished third in their division. They were ready for the playoffs and their chance to defend their title.

In the playoffs, Pittsburgh beat the Washington Capitals, New York Rangers, and Boston Bruins to advance to the finals. Pittsburgh met the Chicago Blackhawks in the Stanley Cup finals. The Blackhawks had been unstoppable early in the playoffs, winning 11 straight games. Instead of being worried about how Chicago was playing, the Penguins remembered that they were defending Cup champions and that they were the best team in the league.

Scotty Bowman took over as coach after the death of Bob Johnson.

GREAT TEAMS IN FOCUS

In Game 1 of the finals, Chicago jumped out to a 3–0 lead. Instead of giving up, the Penguins tried to come back. Phil Bourque scored for Pittsburgh to make it a 3–1 game at the end of the opening period. Chicago scored again in the second, making it a 4–1 game. The Penguins' Lemieux and Rick Tocchet scored late in the second period to bring them within one goal at 4–3. With less than five minutes left in the game, Penguins' star Jagr scored an unbelievable backhand goal, surrounded by three Blackhawk defenders. The game was tied and looked as if it would be heading into overtime. However, with only 13 seconds remaining, Lemieux scored a goal to win the game.

Pittsburgh's Bob Errey scored the first goal of Game 2. Chicago came back in the second period and tied. Lemieux, the Penguins' superstar, took over, scoring two goals to give his team a 3–1 lead. The Penguins' defense then worked extra hard, only allowing Chicago four shots on goal in the last period. They held for a 3–1 win, taking a 2–0 series lead.

Game 3 was a very good defensive game. Penguins' goalie Tom Barrasso stopped all 13 Chicago shots in the first period. Kevin Stevens scored the only goal of the game for Pittsburgh, giving them a 1–0 victory. Facing a sweep, Chicago came out strong in Game 4. They led 3–0 early, but in the third period it was tied at 4–4. Pittsburgh's Stevens and Francis both scored to make it 6–4. Chicago's Jeremy Roenick scored to make it 6–5, but the Blackhawks could not get any closer. Pittsburgh swept the Blackhawks for their second-straight Cup. Lemieux was given the Conn Smythe Trophy, his second year in a row.

More tragedy would keep the Penguins from gaining a third Cup. Lemieux was diagnosed with cancer in January 1993, and though he beat it and returned to the ice that season, he played only 22 games in the next two seasons. Lemieux returned with an excellent individual performance, leading the league in scoring in 1995–1996 and 1996–1997. Sadly, though, he and the Penguins would never again play for the Cup.

1991-1992 Pittsburgh Penguins

Mario Lemieux (1965-)

Mario Lemieux's 199-point season in 1988–1989 and his leadership in the Penguins' two Stanley Cup titles stand out among his greatest moments. But Lemieux will also be remembered for two off-ice achievements that are as important as what he did on the ice.

In 1993 he was diagnosed with Hodgkin's Disease, which is a form of cancer. Two months later, Lemieux was back on the ice, having missed only 23 games. He later took a year off to recover fully. In that time, he found the Mario Lemieux Foundation, which raises money for cancer research.

He also saved the Penguins for the city of Pittsburgh. In 1998 the team went bankrupt and was at risk of moving or folding. The team owed Lemieux more money than it did anyone else, so Lemieux put together an ownership group and bought the team. When he made his comeback in 2000, Lemieux did it as a player and owner.

SAN JOSE SHARKS

First Season: 1991–1992

Franchise Record: 797–710–121–110
Home Rink: SAP Center
(17,483 capacity) in San Jose, California

STANLEY CUPS
None

Joe Pavelski (8)

When the NHL expanded in 1967, California's San Francisco Bay Area got a team. But the Oakland Seals (later, the California Golden Seals) lasted just nine years before moving to Ohio and eventually folding. The league tried the West Coast again in the early 1990s. This time the San Jose Sharks stuck.

Legends & Stars

Evgeni Nabokov

Patrick Marleau	C	1997–present	San Jose made him the second overall draft pick in 1997
Evgeni Nabokov	G	1999–2010	Calder Trophy winner in 2001
Owen Nolan	RW	1995–2003	Five-time All-Star Game selection
Joe Thornton	C	2005–present	NHL's leading scorer and Hart Trophy winner in 2006

By the Numbers

TOP GOAL SCORER 	**Patrick Marleau** 1997–present 437 goals	**TOP GOALTENDER** 	**Evgeni Nabokov** 1999–2010 293 wins
TOP ASSISTS MAN 	**Joe Thornton** 2005–present 567 assists	**TOP DEFENSEMAN** 	**Dan Boyle** 2008–2014 296 points

Third Year's a Charm

The Sharks won just 11 games in their second season, but they made a great leap forward in their third year. In 1993–1994 they went from 24 points in the standings to 82. They ended up going 33-35-16 and made the playoffs. But they weren't done there. In the first round, San Jose upset the top-seeded Red Wings in seven games. In the next series, however, the Sharks lost to the Toronto Maple Leafs in seven games.

Big Trade

Early in the 2005–2006 season, the Sharks pulled off a surprising trade when they got center Joe Thornton from the Boston Bruins. Thornton had been the No. 1 overall draft pick in 1997. He had his best season in his first year at San Jose. He led the NHL in scoring and won the Hart Trophy as MVP. With Thornton, the Sharks became one of the top teams, earning the league's best record in 2008–2009.

Joe Thornton (19)

ST. LOUIS BLUES

First Season: 1967–1968

Franchise Record: 1,625–1,469–432–110
Home Rink: Scottrade Center (19,260 capacity) in St. Louis, Missouri

STANLEY CUPS
None

The St. Louis Blues came into the NHL in the late 1960s when the league doubled in size. They immediately went to three Stanley Cup finals. Much of the success came from the aging but future Hall-of-Fame goalies Glenn Hall and Jacques Plante. The Blues remained regular playoff contenders, thanks to stars Brett Hull, Brian Sutter, and Chris Pronger.

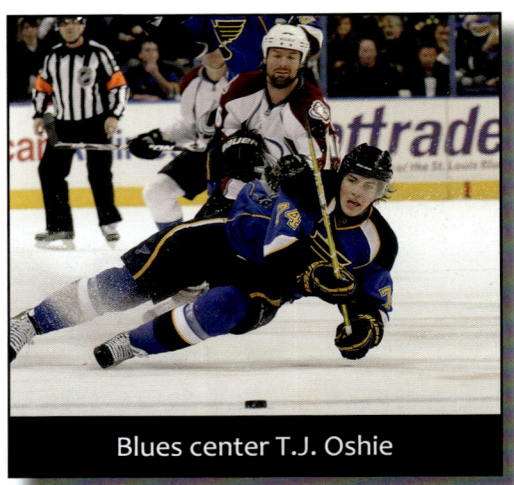
Blues center T.J. Oshie

David Backes

David Backes	C	2006–present	All-Star center led the team in points in 2011–2012
Bernie Federko	C	1976–1989	St. Louis' all-time leading point scorer
Brett Hull	RW	1988–1998	Hart Trophy winner in 1991
Al MacInnis	D	1994–2004	Won the Norris Trophy in 1999
Chris Pronger	D	1995–2004	First defenseman to win the Hart Trophy since Bobby Orr
Brian Sutter	LW	1976–1988	Three-time All-Star played 12 seasons with the Blues

By the Numbers

TOP GOAL SCORER Brett Hull 1988–1998 527 goals

TOP GOALTENDER Mike Liut 1979–1985 151 wins

TOP ASSISTS MAN Bernie Federko 1976–1989 721 assists

TOP DEFENSEMAN Al MacInnis 1994–2004 452 points

Comeback Kids

Two of the best games in Blues history were come-from-behind, 6-5 overtime wins. In 1986 St. Louis pulled off "The Monday Night Miracle," erasing a 5-2 third-period deficit to force a Game 7 in the conference semifinals. In a 2000 regular-season game, the Blues were down 5-0 in the third period and came back to beat the Maple Leafs.

A Stop for "The Great One"

Wayne Gretzky is known as the greatest hockey player of all time. He made his career with the Oilers and the Kings. But he also had a short stint with the Blues, finishing the 1995–1996 season in St. Louis. Gretzky scored 21 points in 18 regular-season games and 16 points in 13 playoff games. But the next season, "The Great One" signed with the New York Rangers and finished his career there.

Wayne Gretzky scores his first goal after being traded to the St. Louis Blues.

TAMPA BAY LIGHTNING

Franchise Record: 652–785–112–109
Home Rink: Tampa Bay Times Forum (19,758 capacity) in Tampa, Florida

STANLEY CUP
2004

First Season: 1992–1993

In 1992 the NHL added two new teams. It put one in the heart of hockey country, Ottawa, which had a team in the league until the 1930s. It put the other along the Gulf Coast of Florida and called it the Tampa Bay Lightning. But the Lightning hasn't played like an outsider. The team has been to the playoffs five times and became the southernmost team in the league to win a championship.

Lightning center Steven Stamkos tied the league lead in goals (51) in 2009–2010.

Legends & Stars

Martin St. Louis

Vincent Lecavalier	C	1998–2013	Four-time All-Star led NHL in goals in 2007
Brad Richards	C	2000–2008	Won Conn Smythe and Lady Byng trophies in 2004
Martin St. Louis	RW	2000–2014	Led NHL in scoring and was Hart Trophy winner in 2004
Steven Stamkos	C	2008–2014	Top draft pick in 2008 led the NHL in goals twice

By the Numbers

TOP GOAL SCORER	Vincent Lecavalier 1998–2013 383 goals	**TOP GOALTENDER**	Nikolai Khabibulin 2000–2004 83 wins
TOP ASSISTS MAN	Martin St. Louis 2000–2014 588 assists	**TOP DEFENSEMAN**	Dan Boyle 2002–2008 253 points

Magical Season

The Lightning had many heroes on their way to winning the Stanley Cup in 2004. Goalie Nikolai Khabibulin had five shutouts and Brad Richards scored 12 goals in the playoffs. League MVP Martin St. Louis scored a double-overtime goal in Game 6 of the finals. Ruslan Fedotenko scored both Tampa Bay goals in the Game 7 clincher.

2004 Stanley Cup champions

Famous First

In 1992 the Lightning made history when they signed goaltender Manon Rheaume. She was the first and only woman to play in the NHL. However, her only appearance came during an exhibition game.

TORONTO MAPLE LEAFS

First Season: 1917–1918

Franchise Record: 2,735–2,623–783–109
Home Rink: Air Canada Centre (18,800 capacity) in Toronto, Ontario, Canada

STANLEY CUPS
1918, 1922, 1932, 1942, 1945, 1947, 1948, 1949, 1951, 1962, 1963, 1964, 1967

Toronto's NHL team was first known as the Arenas. They won a Stanley Cup under that nickname and another as the St. Pats before the legendary Conn Smythe took over the team in the 1920s. He changed the name to the Maple Leafs, after Canada's Maple Leaf Regiment that fought in World War I. Toronto captured 11 titles after the name change. The team has not reached the finals since winning the Cup in 1967.

Maple Leafs center Nik Antropov (11) played more than eight seasons with Toronto.

Legends & Stars

Tomas Kaberle

Syl Apps	C	1936–1943, 1945–1948	Led Toronto to three titles in the 1940s
Turk Broda	G	1936–1952	Two-time Vezina Trophy winner and five-time Cup winner
Hap Day		1940–1950	Toronto coach led the Leafs to five championships
Tim Horton	D	1949–1970	Seven-time All-Star Game participant
Punch Imlach		1958–1969, 1979–1980	Leafs' coach won four Cups, including a "three-peat" in the 1960s
Tomas Kaberle	D	1998–2011	Selected to the All-Star Game four times
Ted Kennedy	C	1942–1955, 1956–1957	Won the Hart Trophy in 1955
Dave Keon	C	1960–1975	Eight-time All-Star won the Conn Smythe Trophy in 1967
Phil Kessel	C	2009–present	Two-time All-Star led the team in points five straight years
Frank Mahovlich	LW	1956–1968	"The Big M" led the Leafs to four Stanley Cup wins

By the Numbers

TOP GOAL SCORER — Mats Sundin, 1994–2008, 420 goals

TOP GOALTENDER — Turk Broda, 1936–1952, 302 wins

TOP ASSISTS MAN — Borje Salming, 1973–1989, 620 assists

TOP DEFENSEMAN — Tim Horton, 1949–1970, 1,185 games played

More Hall of Famers

Of the more than 350 people inducted in the Hockey Hall of Fame, more than 50 have been part of the Maple Leafs organization. That's more than any other team in the NHL. Fittingly, the Hall of Fame is located in Toronto—Canada's largest city.

Playing Hurt

Bob Baun might not be one of the Maple Leafs' greatest players, but he sure is a legend. In Game 6 of the 1964 Stanley Cup finals, a puck was shot and hit Baun, breaking his foot. He was taken off the ice on a stretcher, but he returned for overtime. With his foot numbed and taped, Baun scored the game-winning goal. Two nights later, Toronto won Game 7 and their third-straight Stanley Cup.

GREAT TEAMS IN FOCUS

1966-1967 TORONTO MAPLE LEAFS

Few teams are remembered as fondly in their home city as the 1966–1967 Toronto Maple Leafs. It was the last season for many of the team's popular players, who were getting ready to retire. The goalies were 42-year-old Johnny Bower and 37-year-old Terry Sawchuck. Three key players—Red Kelly, Bob Pulford, and George "Chief" Armstrong—were all 39 years old. Coach Punch Imlach had to take time off to rest during the season. However, the Maple Leafs finished third and faced the league's best team, the Chicago Blackhawks, in the semifinals. Bower was injured during Game 5, and Sawchuck took his place. Sawchuck had 49 saves in 40 minutes as the Maple Leafs won and moved on to the finals against the Montreal Canadiens.

Two Canadian teams would battle for the championship. The Maple Leafs and Canadiens had been the champions in 18 of the past 24 seasons, so it was no surprise to find them facing each other. The Canadiens entered the final series on a 15-game unbeaten streak. In Game 1 Sawchuck started in goal for the Maple Leafs and couldn't stop the Canadiens as they scored four goals against him. The Canadiens rolled to a 6–2 victory. Coach Imlach wasn't pleased with Sawchuck's performance and started Bower in goal for Game 2. It was a good decision. Bower stopped all 31 shots he faced, and the Maple Leafs won 3–0 behind goals from Pete Stemkowski, Mike Walton, and Tim Horton. The series was tied at 1–1.

Terry Sawchuck watches as the Canadiens threaten to score in Game 1 of the Stanley Cup.

Game 3 was a great defensive game by both goalies. Bower faced 63 shots on goal and gave up only two. The game stretched into overtime, and then it went into double overtime. Toronto's Pulford scored the game-winning goal. Before Game 4, Bower hurt his leg, and

Great Teams in Focus

1966-1967 Record

Won	Lost	Tied	Playoffs
32	27	11	Defeated Chicago Blackhawks 4–2
			Defeated Montreal Canadiens 4–2

the Maple Leafs were forced to start Sawchuck, who once again could not stop the Canadiens. He allowed six goals, which gave Montreal a 6–2 victory. The series was tied again, at 2–2.

Surprisingly, Sawchuck started Game 5. This time, however, he was ready to play. The first two periods of the game, he dove all over the ice, stopping every shot that came near him. Toronto scored three goals in the second period and broke the game open. In the third period, Toronto's defense was great, as they made it hard for the Canadiens to shoot and pass near their goal. They held on to win 4–1, coming within one win of the Stanley Cup.

Coach Imlach stuck with Sawchuck for Game 6, and the goalie stopped all 17 first period shots against him. Ron Ellis and Jim Pappin scored in the second period, giving the Maple Leafs a 2–0 lead. The Canadiens came back and scored a goal, making it 2–1. In the final minute, with the Canadiens threatening

Dave Koen attacks the goal during the 1967 Stanley Cup finals.

to score, a face-off was called in Toronto's zone. Coach Imlach made a daring move and sent in an all-veteran lineup. Once again, his coaching proved to be great, and Allan Stanley, age 41, won the face-off against Montreal's star Jean Beliveau. George Armstrong broke away for a goal, and the Leafs clinched a 3–1 victory. This made them champions for the fourth time in six years. It was their 13th Stanley Cup.

VANCOUVER CANUCKS

First Season: 1970–1971

Franchise Record: 1,415–1,504–391–100
Home Rink: Rogers Arena (18,630 capacity) in Vancouver, British Columbia, Canada

STANLEY CUPS
None

It took many years for the NHL to arrive in Vancouver, British Columbia. However, Canada's third-largest city had a long history with professional hockey before 1970. In 1915 a team called the Vancouver Millionaires played in the Pacific Coast Hockey Association. The Millionaires even won the Stanley Cup. As for the Canucks, they are still waiting to win their first championship.

Canucks center Ryan Kesler in the 2009 NHL playoffs

Legends & Stars

Roberto Luongo

Trevor Linden	RW	1988–1998, 2001–2008	Two-time All-Star Game selection
Roberto Luongo	G	2006–2014	Played in three All-Star Games
Markus Naslund	LW	1996–2008	Won the Lester B. Pearson Award in 2003
Daniel Sedin	LW	2000–present	Two-time All-Star led the NHL in points in 2010–2011
Henrik Sedin	C	2000–present	2010 league MVP is Vancouver's all-time points leader
Stan Smyl	RW	1978–1991	Was the Canucks' leading scorer upon retiring after 13 seasons

By the Numbers

TOP GOAL SCORER	Markus Naslund 1996–2008 346 goals	**TOP GOALTENDER**	Roberto Luongo 2006–2014 252 wins
TOP ASSISTS MAN	Henrik Sedin 2000–present 649 assists	**TOP DEFENSEMAN**	Dennis Kearns 1971–1981 290 assists

Working Overtime

During the Canucks' run to the 1994 Stanley Cup finals, they won seven overtime games. In the first round Vancouver trailed the Flames three games to one before winning three straight overtime games. Star forward Pavel Bure scored the double-overtime goal in Game 7 to send the Canucks to the championship series.

Twin Engines

In 1999 the Canucks made a trade to secure the second- and third-overall selections in the NHL draft. They used those picks to draft twin brothers Daniel and Henrik Sedin. The two have played on the same line together ever since. In 2009 they each signed a new contract to stay in Vancouver—and stay together. The twins are the franchise's top two scorers, both compiling more than 800 career points.

Daniel Sedin (22) and Henrik Sedin (33)

WASHINGTON CAPITALS

First Season: 1974–1975

Franchise Record: 1,370–1,317–303–108

Home Rink: Verizon Center (18,277 capacity) in Washington, D.C.

STANLEY CUPS
None

With such players as Alex Ovechkin and Nicklas Backstrom, the Washington Capitals are one of the most exciting teams in the NHL. It wasn't always that way though. They won just eight games in their first season. At one point they lost 17 games in a row. But since cracking the playoffs in the early 1980s, they've seldom been left out of the postseason.

Capitals goalie Semyon Varlamov defends the net during the 2009 playoffs.

Legends & Stars

Nicklas Backstrom

Name	Pos	Years	Notes
Nicklas Backstrom	C	2007–present	2008 All-Rookie selection
Peter Bondra	RW	1990–2004	Five-time All-Star Game pick
Mike Gartner	RW	1979–1989	Seven-time All-Star Game selection
Dale Hunter	C	1987–1999	Ranks second all-time in penalty minutes
Rod Langway	D	1982–1993	Six-time All-Star Game pick and two-time Norris Trophy winner
Alex Ovechkin	LW	2005–present	Won Hart Trophy as MVP in 2008, 2009, and 2013

By the Numbers

TOP GOAL SCORER	Peter Bondra 1990–2004 472 goals	**TOP GOALTENDER**	Olaf Kolzig 1989–2008 301 wins
TOP ASSISTS MAN	Michal Pivonka 1986–1999 418 assists	**TOP DEFENSEMAN**	Calle Johansson 1989–2003 474 points

Alexander the Great

During his Calder Trophy-winning season, Alex Ovechkin scored what Capitals fans refer to as simply "the goal." Falling on the ice with his back to the goal and his hands above his head, the superstar still found a way to shoot the puck and put it in the net. Two years later, in 2008, Ovechkin became the first player to win the Hart, Ross, Pearson, and Richard trophies all in the same season.

Ironman Streak

Doug Jarvis started his career with the Montreal Canadiens in 1975 and ended it with the Hartford Whalers in 1987. In between he spent four seasons with the Capitals. Along the way, Jarvis never missed a game and set the NHL's consecutive-game streak of 964.

WINNIPEG JETS

First Season: 1999–2000

Franchise Record: 440-528-45-101
Home Rink: MTS Centre (15,004 capacity) in Winnipeg, Manitoba, Canada

STANLEY CUPS
None

The Winnipeg Jets began life south of the border as the Atlanta Thrashers. After 11 seasons in Georgia, the team headed north in 2012 and became the Winnipeg Jets. The Jets take their name from Winnipeg's original NHL team, which moved to Arizona in 1996 to become the Coyotes.

Evander Kane

Legends & Stars

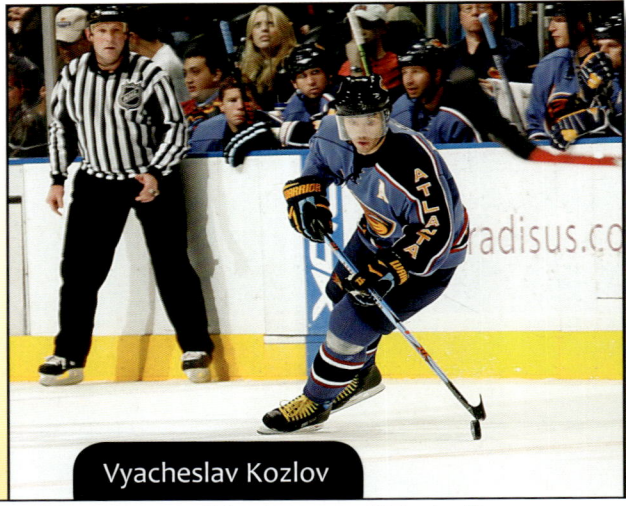
Vyacheslav Kozlov

Evander Kane	LW	2009–present	Selected fourth overall in the 2009 NHL draft
Ilya Kovalchuk	LW	2001–2010	No. 1 overall draft pick in 2001 led the team in scoring and assists
Vyacheslav Kozlov	LW	2002–2010	Longtime Red Wings star had eight game-winning goals during the 2006–2007 season
Kari Lehtonen	G	2003–2009	Led the team in career shutouts with 14

By the Numbers

TOP GOAL SCORER
Ilya Kovalchuk
2001–2010
328 goals

TOP GOALTENDER
Ondrej Pavelec
2007–present
113 wins

TOP ASSISTS MAN
Ilya Kovalchuk
287 assists

TOP DEFENSEMAN
Tobias Enstrom
2007–present
249 points

Searching for Success

The Jets have made the playoffs just once in their 14-year history. Led by 100-point scorer Marian Hossa, they went as the Thrashers in 2007 after winning the Southeast Division. However, they were knocked out in the first round by the New York Rangers.

Marian Hossa

Jets Take Off

When it was announced that the NHL was returning to Winnipeg in 2011, the team had hopes that it could sell 13,000 season tickets. No problem. Fans who had waited 15 years for a team to come back to Manitoba bought up the tickets in just 17 minutes. The Jets keep a season-ticket waiting list of 8,000 fans.

1960–2014 STANLEY CUP WINNERS

1960–1961	Chicago Blackhawks
1961–1962	Toronto Maple Leafs
1962–1963	Toronto Maple Leafs
1963–1964	Toronto Maple Leafs
1964–1965	Montreal Canadiens
1965–1966	Montreal Canadiens
1966–1967	Toronto Maple Leafs
1967–1968	Montreal Canadiens
1968–1969	Montreal Canadiens
1969–1970	Boston Bruins
1970–1971	Montreal Canadiens
1971–1972	Boston Bruins
1972–1973	Montreal Canadiens
1973–1974	Philadelphia Flyers
1974–1975	Philadelphia Flyers
1975–1976	Montreal Canadiens
1976–1977	Montreal Canadiens
1977–1978	Montreal Canadiens
1978–1979	Montreal Canadiens
1979–1980	New York Islanders
1980–1981	New York Islanders
1981–1982	New York Islanders
1982–1983	New York Islanders
1983–1984	Edmonton Oilers
1984–1985	Edmonton Oilers
1985–1986	Montreal Canadiens
1986–1987	Edmonton Oilers
1987–1988	Edmonton Oilers

1988–1989	Calgary Flames		2002–2003	New Jersey Devils
1989–1990	Edmonton Oilers		2003–2004	Tampa Bay Lightning
1990–1991	Pittsburgh Penguins		2004–2005	No champion due to lockout
1991–1992	Pittsburgh Penguins		2005–2006	Carolina Hurricanes
1992–1993	Montreal Canadiens		2006–2007	Anaheim Ducks
1993–1994	New York Rangers		2007–2008	Detroit Red Wings
1994–1995	New Jersey Devils		2008–2009	Pittsburgh Penguins
1995–1996	Colorado Avalanche		2009–2010	Chicago Blackhawks
1996–1997	Detroit Red Wings		2010–2011	Boston Bruins
1997–1998	Detroit Red Wings		2011–2012	Los Angeles Kings
1998–1999	Dallas Stars		2012–2013	Chicago Blackhawks
1999–2000	New Jersey Devils		2013–2014	Los Angeles Kings
2000–2001	Colorado Avalanche			
2001–2002	Detroit Red Wings			

GLOSSARY

assist pass that leads to a goal; as many as two assists can be awarded on one goal

body check when a player uses a hip or shoulder to bump an opponent off the puck

conference grouping in hockey; teams are grouped into two conferences—the Eastern Conference and the Western Conference

dynasty team that wins multiple championships over a period of several years

face-off dropping the puck between two players to restart play

franchise team that operates under the rules and regulations of a professional sports league or organization

hat trick three goals in one game

MVP (Most Valuable Player) hockey award given to the player who helps his or her team the most. In the NHL, the actual award is called the Hart Trophy.

National Hockey League (NHL) professional hockey league that was founded in 1917. As of 2015, there were 30 teams in the NHL.

overtime extra period played if the score is tied at the end of a game

period division in a hockey game; a hockey game is divided into three 20-minute periods

power play when a player serves a penalty, the opposing team has a one-person advantage, usually for two minutes or until the team on the power play scores

rookie first-year player

seed how a team is ranked for the Stanley Cup playoffs, based on the team's regular season record and point total

shootout method of breaking a tie score at the end of overtime play

shutout game in which one team fails to score a goal

Stanley Cup silver trophy awarded to the NHL champions

sweep winning all of the games in a series

veteran older, more experienced player

World Hockey Association (WHA) professional hockey league that was created in 1972 to compete with the NHL. The WHA merged with the NHL in the 1979–1980 season.

HOCKEY POSITIONS

center (C) forward who plays in the middle of the rink

defenseman (D) one of two players who stays by the ice's blue line to help defend his or her goal

goaltender (G) player who plays in front of the net and tries to stop the other team from scoring

left wing (LW) forward who plays on the left side of the rink

right wing (RW) forward who plays on the right side of the rink

NHL AWARD TROPHIES

Art Ross Trophy leading point scorer

Bill Masterton Memorial Trophy player who displays perseverance and dedication to hockey

Calder Memorial Trophy rookie of the year

Conn Smythe Trophy most valuable player of the playoffs

Frank J. Selke Trophy top defensive forward

Hart Memorial Trophy most valuable player

Jack Adams Award coach of the year

James Norris Memorial Trophy top defenseman

King Clancy Memorial Trophy player who displays leadership on the ice and in the community

Lady Byng Memorial Trophy player who displays gentlemanly conduct

Lester B. Pearson Award MVP as voted on by the players

Maurice "Rocket" Richard Trophy leading goal-scorer

Vezina Trophy top goaltender

William M. Jennings Trophy goaltender with the lowest goals-against average

READ MORE

Frederick, Shane. *The Technology of Hockey.* Sports Illustrated Kids. North Mankato, Minn.: Capstone Press, 2013.

Frederick, Shane. *The Ultimate Collection of Pro Hockey Records 2015.* Sports Illustrated Kids. North Mankato, Minn.: Capstone Press, 2014.

Goldner, John. *Hockey Talk: The Language of Hockey from A–Z.* Markham, Ontario: Fitzhenry & Whiteside, 2010.

Weekes, Don. *World Class Trivia.* Vancouver, BC: Greystone Books, 2009.

INTERNET SITES

FactHound offers a safe, fun way to find Internet sites related to this book. All of the sites on FactHound have been researched by our staff.

Here's all you do:

Visit www.facthound.com

Type in this code: 9781491419632

INDEX

Adams, Jack 50, 55
Alfredsson, Daniel 94, 95
Anaheim Ducks 22–23, 95
Anderson, Craig 94
Anderson, Glenn 56, 58, 59
Antropov, Nik 110
Apps, Syl 18, 110
Arizona Coyotes 24–25
Armstrong, George 112, 113
Arnott, Jason 78
Atlanta Thrashers 118

Babych, Dave 37
Backes, David 106
Backstrom, Niklas 66, 67, 116
Barber, Bill 96, 97
Barrasso, Tom 102
Bathgate, Andy 88
Baun, Bob 111
Belfour, Ed 48, 49
Beliveau, Jean 68, 69, 70, 71, 72, 113
Bergeron, Patrice 26
best-of-seven series 8
Blake, Hector 68
Blake, Rob 43, 64, 65
Blake, Toe 70
Bobrovsky, Sergei 46
Bondra, Peter 116, 117
Bossy, Mike 12, 82, 83, 84, 86, 87
Boston Bruins 5, 10, 14, 20–21, 26–31, 64, 75, 76–77, 96, 97, 101
Bouchard, Emile 11
Boucher, Brian 25
Boucher, Frank 88
Bourque, Phil 102
Bourque, Ray 26, 27, 42–43, 45
Bouwmeester, Jay 62
Bower, Johnny 112
Bowman, Scotty 68, 74, 101
Boyle, Dan 105, 109
Brimsek, Frank 26
Brind'Amour, Rod 36
Broda, Turk 18, 110, 111
Brodeur, Martin 80, 81
Broten, Neal 48
Brunette, Andrew 67
Bryzgalov, Ilya 25
Bucyk, John 26, 27, 29, 30
Buffalo Sabres 32–33, 49
Bure, Pavel 62, 115
Burns, Brent 67

Calgary Flames 34–35, 59, 115
California Golden Seals 46, 104
Carolina Hurricanes 36–37
Cashman, Wayne 30
Cecil, Brittanie 47
"Challenge Cup Era" 7
Chara, Zdeno 20, 26
Cheevers, Gerry 29, 76
Chelios, Chris 38
Chicago Blackhawks 5, 29, 38–39, 91, 101–102, 112
Clarke, Bobby 96, 97
Cleveland Barons 75
Coffey, Paul 56, 57, 59, 99
Colorado Avalanche 40–45, 48, 63, 67
Colorado Rockies 40, 80
Columbia Blue Jackets 46–47
Cook, Bill 88
Cournoyer, Yvan 14, 69, 74
Crosby, Sidney 98, 99
Curry, Floyd 72

Dallas Stars 48–49
Daneyko, Ken 80
Day, Hap 18, 110
Delvecchio, Alex 50, 53, 54, 55
Detroit Red Wings 5, 8, 10, 14, 18, 37, 50–55, 69, 72
Detroit Vipers 52
Dionne, Marcel 64, 65
Doan, Shane 24
Doughty, Drew 64
Drury, Chris 43, 45
Dryden, Ken 68, 74, 76

Eastern Conference 8
Edmonton Oilers 10, 14–15, 16–17, 37, 43, 56–61, 65
Elias, Patrik 80, 81
Elliott, Brian 94
Ellis, Ron 113
Enstrom, Tobias 119
Eriksson, Loui 48
Errey, Bob 102
Esposito, Phil 26, 28, 29, 31
Esposito, Tony 38, 39

Federko, Bernie 106, 107
Fedorov, Sergei 50
Fedotenko, Ruslan 109
female player 109
Finnigan, Frank 95
Fleury, Marc-Andre 99
Fleury, Theoren 34
Florida Panthers 62–63
Foote, Adam 41, 45
Forsberg, Peter 40, 41, 42
Francis, Ron 36, 37, 98, 100, 102
Fuhr, Grant 16, 56, 57, 58, 59

Gaborik, Marian 66, 67
Gagne, Simon 96
Gainey, Bob 74
Gartner, Mike 116
Geoffrion, Bernie 55, 70, 72
Giguere, Jean-Sebastien 23
Gilbert, Rod 89
Gillies, Clark 59, 82, 84, 86
Giroux, Claude 96
Graves, Adam 90
Gretzky, Wayne 5, 14, 15, 25, 52, 56, 57, 58, 60, 61, 64, 65, 100, 107
Grier, Mike 32

Hall, Glenn 38, 106
Hall of Fame 12, 18, 41, 45, 58, 70, 74, 88, 89, 99, 106, 111
Hall, Taylor 56
Harvey, Doug 68, 70
Hasek, Dominik 32
Hawerchuk, Dale 24, 25
Heatley, Dany 94
Hejduk, Milan 40
Hextall, Ron 97
Hinote, Dan 43
Horton, Nathan 62
Horton, Tim 110, 111, 112
Hossa, Marian 119
Housley, Phil 33
Howe, Gordie 5, 14, 37, 50, 51, 52, 53, 54, 55, 72, 100
Howe, Mark 37, 97
Howe, Marty 37
Hull, Bobby 24, 38, 39, 85
Hull, Brett 48, 49, 106, 107
Hunter, Dale 116

Iginla, Jarome 34, 35
Imlach, Punch 110, 112, 113

Jagr, Jaromir 98, 100, 102
Jarvis, Doug 117
Johansson, Calle 117
Jokinen, Olli 63

Kaberle, Tomas 110
Kamensky, Valeri 41
Kane, Evander 118
Kane, Patrick 38
Kansas City Scouts 80
Karakas, Mike 39
Kariya, Paul 22
Kearns, Dennis 115
Keenan, Larry 31
Keenan, Mike 90, 91
Kelly, Red 50, 72, 112
Kennedy, Ted 110
Keon, Dave 110
Kesler, Ryan 114
Kessel, Phil 110
Khabibulin, Nikolai 109
Kiprusoff, Miikka 34, 35
Klesla, Rostislav 46
Koen, Dave 113
Koivu, Mikko 66, 67
Kolzig, Olaf 117
Kopecky, Tomas 8
Kovalchuk, Ilya 118, 119
Kozlov, Vyacheslav 118
Kurri, Jari 56, 58, 60

Lafleur, Guy 68, 69, 72, 74, 75, 77
LaFontaine, Pat 32, 83
Lalime, Patrick 95
Lambert, Yvon 76
Langway, Rod 116
Lapointe, Guy 74
Lecavalier, Vincent 108, 109
Leetch, Brian 88, 89, 90
Legwand, David 79
Lehtonen, Kari 118
Lemaire, Jacques 14, 74, 77
Lemieux, Claude 41, 80
Lemieux, Mario 5, 14, 58, 98, 99, 100, 102, 103
Lidstrom, Nicklas 50, 51
Linden, Trevor 114
Lindros, Eric 96
Lindsay, Ted 50, 53, 54, 72
Linseman, Ken 60
Liut, Mike 107
Los Angeles Kings 43, 61, 64–65
Lundqvist, Henrik 88, 89
Luongo, Roberto 21, 63, 114, 115

McClelland, Kevin 59
McDonald, Lanny 35
MacInnis, Al 34, 35, 106, 107
McKenzie, John 30
McNeil, Gerry 11
MacTavish, Craig 56
Mahovlich, Frank 110
Malkin, Evgeni 98
Marleau, Patrick 104, 105
Martin, Rick 32, 33
Mason, Steve 46, 47
Mellanby, Scott 63
Messier, Mark 17, 18, 56, 57, 59, 89, 90, 92, 93
Mikita, Stan 38, 39
Miller, Ryan 32, 33
Minnesota North Stars 48, 49, 59, 66, 67
Minnesota Wild 66–67
Modano, Mike 48, 49
Montreal Amateur Athletics Association 6
Montreal Canadiens 5, 10, 11, 14, 39, 44, 53–55, 68–77, 112–113, 117
Morenz, Howie 68
Moss, David 34

Nabokov, Evgeni 104, 105
Nash, Rick 46, 47
Nashville Predators 78–79
Naslund, Markus 114, 115
National Hockey Association (NHA) 7
National Hockey League (NHL)
formation 7
season 8
Neely, Cam 26
"neutral-zone trap" 43
New England Whalers 36
New Jersey Devils 23, 40, 42, 43, 45, 80–81, 92

127

INDEX

New York Islanders 12–13, 14, 58, 59–60, 76, 77, 82–7, 92
New York Rangers 5, 18–19, 29, 72, 84, 86, 88–93, 101, 119
Niedermayer, Rob 23
Niedermayer, Scott 22, 23, 81
Nieminen, Ville 45
Nieuwendyk, Joe 48
Nolan, Owen 104
Numminen, Teppo 24, 25
Nystrom, Bob 13, 83, 86

Oakland Seals 104
Olmstead, Bert 70
O'Ree, Willie 27
"Original Six" 5, 64, 90
Orr, Bobby 5, 26, 27, 28, 29, 30, 31
Osgood, Chris 50
Oshie, T.J. 106
Ottawa Senators 94–95
Ovechkin, Alex 116, 117

Pacific Coast Hockey Association (PCHA) 7
Pappin, Jim 113
Parent, Bernie 96
Parise, J.P. 67
Parise, Zach 66, 67, 80
Park, Brad 88
Patrick, Lester 88
Pavelec, Ondrej 119
Pavelich, Marty 54
Pavelski, Joe 104
Perreault, Gilbert 32, 33
Perry, Corey 22
Philadelphia Flyers 16–17, 33, 81, 83, 91, 96–97
Pilote, Pierre 38
Pittsburgh Penguins 14, 33, 85, 86, 98–103
Pivonka, Michal 117
Plante, Jacques 68, 69, 70, 106
Poile, David 79
Pollack, Sam 74
Portland Rosebuds 38
Potvin, Denis 82, 83, 84
Poulin, Dave 17

Price, Carey 68
Pronger, Chris 106
Pronovost, Marcel 54
Provost, Claude 72
Pulford, Bob 112

Quebec Nordiques 40, 41, 86
Quick, Jonathan 64, 65

Redden, Wade 95
Reibel, Earl 55
Reinprecht, Steven 43
Rheaume, Manon 109
Richard, Henri 69
Richard, Maurice 10, 68, 69, 70, 100
Richards, Brad 108, 109
Richter, Mike 90
Rinne, Pekka 78, 79
Robert, René 33
Robinson, Larry 68, 69, 74
Robitaille, Luc 64, 65
Roenick, Jeremy 24, 102
Ross, Art 26
Roy, Patrick 40, 41, 42, 43, 44, 45, 67
Ryder, Michael 21

St. Louis, Martin 108, 109
St. Louis Blues 29–31, 43, 76, 77, 91, 106–107
Sakic, Joe 40, 41, 42, 43, 45
Salming, Borje 111
San Jose Sharks 104–105
Sather, Glen 56, 58
Savard, Denis 38
Savard, Serge 74, 76
Sawchuck, Terry 42, 50, 51, 53, 69, 112, 113
Schmautz, Bobby 77
Schultz, Dave 97
Schutt, Steve 74, 75, 76
Sedin, Daniel 114, 115
Sedin, Henrik 114, 115
Selanne, Teemu 22, 23
Selke, Frank 70
Shero, Fred 96
Shore, Eddie 26, 27
Skoula, Martin 43
Smith, Billy 59, 82, 83, 84
Smyl, Stan 114

Smythe, Conn 110
Spezza, Jason 94
Staal, Eric 36, 37
Stamkos, Steven 108
Stanley, Allan 113
Stanley Cup 6–7, 8
Stanley Cup winners 122–123
Stastny, Paul 40, 41
Stastny, Peter 40, 41
Steen, Thomas 25
Stemkowski, Pete 112
Stevens, Kevin 102
Stevens, Scott 80
Subban, P.K. 68
Sullivan, Steve 78
Sundin, Mats 111
Suter, Ryan 66, 67
Sutter, Brent 35
Sutter, Brett 35
Sutter, Brian 35, 106
Sutter, Darryl 35
Sutter, Ron 35
Svehla, Robert 63

Tampa Bay Lightning 108–109
Tanguay, Alex 45
Tavares, John 82
Thomas, Tim 26
Thompson, Tiny 27
Thornton, Joe 104, 105
Tkachuk, Keith 24
Tocchet, Rick 102
Toews, Jonathan 38
Tonelli, John 85
Tootoo, Jordin 79
Toronto Maple Leafs 5, 10, 11, 18, 39, 53, 55, 72, 105, 107, 110–113
Torres, Raffi 46
Tremblay, Mario 44, 76
Trottier, Bryan 12, 13, 82, 83, 84
Trotz, Barry 79
Turco, Marty 48, 49
Tyutin, Fedor 47

Umberger, R.J. 46

Vanbiesbrouck, John 62, 63
Vancouver Canucks 18, 20–21, 43, 86, 93, 114–115
Vancouver Millionaires 114
Varlamov, Semyon 116
Verbeek, Pat 49
Vokoun, Tomas 78

Walton, Mike 112
Walz, Wes 66
Ward, Cam 36, 37

Washington Capitals 92, 101, 116–117
Weber, Shea 78, 79
Weiss, Stephen 62, 63
Western Conference 8
wild card teams 8
Wilson, Doug 39
Winnipeg Jets 24, 59, 118–119
Winter Classics 33
World Hockey Association (WHA) 24, 36, 52, 85
Worsley, Gump 88

Yzerman, Steve 50, 51

Zubov, Sergei 49, 90